Carol

W9-CLV-499

THE BIG BOOK OF SMALL NEEDLEWORK GIFTS

by Annette Feldman

Edited by Jeanne McClow

Photography by Doug Long, Photocraft

A Rutledge Book

HAMMOND®
INCORPORATED
MAPLEWOOD, NEW JERSEY 07040

*Dedicated
to
The Memory of My Parents,
Gertrude and Emanuel Gerber,
and to
Irving Feldman, My Husband,
Harold E. Grove, My First Editor and Now My Good Friend,
Valerie Kurita, My Assistant and Close Associate,
and
"My Hands," Without Whom This Book
Would Not Have Been Possible:
Antonia Builes, Marjorie Williams, Julie Burgess,
Bertha Zeltser, Julia Nemar,
Janet McEneaney, and Michelle Hines.*

*Special thanks also to
Deborah Weiss.*

Prepared and produced by Rutledge Books, Inc., New York, New York

Published by Hammond, Inc., 515 Valley Street, Maplewood, New Jersey 07040

First edition 1980
Printed in the United States of America

ISBN 0-8437-3360-8

Library of Congress Cataloging in Publication Data

Feldman, Annette.
   The big book of small needlework gifts.

   "A Rutledge book."
   Includes index.
   1. Needlework. 2. Gifts. I. McClow, Jeanne.
II. Title.
TT715.F44   746.4   80-16499

Contents

Introduction

I've created the new designs in this book with the knowledge that it's fun to both give and receive presents and, beyond that, with the desire to share some of that fun with you. Of the approximately eighty gift ideas appearing on the pages that follow, of which some are parts of two- and three-piece sets that can be made separately, about half have been created with little people in mind and the rest are for big people. All are quite different from anything you've ever given before, first because they've been designed specifically for this book and cannot be found anywhere else, and then because each will be a new thing that you have made yourself with your own choice of colors and fabrics. For these reasons, whatever gifts you decide to make will certainly be received as something very special by whomever you've decided to make them for and will be appreciated as presents that were actually made just for them.

Whether you knit, crochet, or sew, you will find very unusual things here to interest you. Some of the designs are whimsical whereas others are very fashionable, and all are relatively simple to make just by following the easy step-by-step instructions that accompany each new project. For the little people, there are, for fun, small, cuddly, terry crib toys that rattle when you shake them, a fake-fur puppy that is very lovable, and very real-looking, and doll's clothes and soft furnishings for a dollhouse to be played with for hour upon hour, as many little people enjoy doing. For fashion for the youngsters, there is a black, multistriped, two-piece yoga suit with matching espadrilles for a two-year-old who will discover the feeling of being sophisticated the minute he puts on the outfit and long, old-fashioned-looking, striped swim trunks for a little "him," with her counterpart being a two-piece bikini outfit with a pair of spare pants—clamdiggers this time—for when the sun goes down. For big people, where fun and fashion are often one and the same, there is for her, among other things, a metallic cloth obi sash, a six-foot-long, skinny boa crocheted with glittery yarn, and an oversized, monogrammed mohair beret; for him there is an under-or-over-the-shirt Norwegian thermal slipover; and for anyone who plays a guitar, a very attractive, knitted guitar strap is just the thing.

I've derived a great deal of pleasure from working on this collection of new designs, and I sincerely hope that you will have as much pleasure in making them. Your choice of colors and fabrics will add even more to the uniqueness of whatever you have chosen to make, and actually—I guess it should not be kept a secret—it's quite all right if you should decide to keep some of the things you've made as presents for yourself instead of giving them all away to others. After all, why not?

Let Your Gift Look Handmade, Not Homemade

Accompanying all the new designer gifts that appear in the pages of this book are the paragraphs that tell you how to make them. The instructions in these paragraphs are clear and easy to follow. If you read them with care, you should have no problem in being able to re-create as many of the beautiful things as you choose, with your own two hands and in the comfort of your own easy chair. Those who are accustomed to doing handwork already know what a great source of pleasure this can be and what a sense of fulfillment there is when your project has finally been completed. Those of you who are new at handcrafts will discover a wonderful addition to your life-style, a hobby that is interesting, creative, calming, and all-absorbing, yet one that doesn't prevent you in any way from participating in conversation with others or in following a good story on television.

The pieces we have designed for you are either crocheted, knitted, or sewn, and many of them are re-embroidered. While the minimum amount of effort with which you can make any one of them will belie the beauty of your finished work, there are certain ground rules that your should know in order to be really proud of that finished piece. "Heart" and tender, loving hands are not quite enough to achieve the perfect handmade look you want instead of something that looks a little homemade and is just not quite right. Some of the rules, as a matter of fact, are the same simple ones that apply to making a cake, pie, or hearty soup. Just as it is important in the making of these to read quickly through your recipe first to know what ingredients you will need, to see that whatever equipment you will be using is in good order, to measure accurately, and to take the time and patience to do the job right, so it is absolutely necessary that you follow those procedures in the working of your handicraft project. In addition, you should be aware of certain special techniques in needlework that will make it possible to get the perfect finish you would like. To help you avoid these and many other unnecessary problems, we have written the paragraphs that follow and hope you will read them and learn from them the "how-to" of needlework perfection.

General Rules for All Handwork

After selecting the pattern you want to make, draw up a list of all the materials required. Then select them with care, being certain that you are buying a sufficient amount of yarn or fabric so that you will not run short and be faced with the problem of not being able to buy more of the same dye lot. Also be sure that the material is of a good-enough quality to stand up well and warrant the effort you will be putting into your work. See that your scissors, needles, and other working tools are sharp and in otherwise good condition in order to facilitate your work. Then, with everything on hand, find your "easy chair" working space in a well-lighted, comfortable area of your home. You will then be able to start your project with a quiet, calm feeling of assurance that your are about to begin something that will one day justify your anticipation and will turn out to be a creation of your own that you will be very proud of.

Enlarging and Transferring Patterns

A number of the sewing and embroidery projects in this book will require enlarging and/or transferring patterns. Each of those to be enlarged will be overlaid with a grid, each square of which equals one inch or two inches. To enlarge the piece, simply draw on a large piece of brown wrapping (or other) paper a grid containing the same number of squares—making each square one inch or two inches, according to the pattern instructions. Then copy the pattern square by square onto the paper. To transfer a design, trace the design in the book. Then place dressmaker's tracing paper, carbon-side down, on the right side of the fabric, lay the traced design on top, and then trace over it with a pencil. Take care to hold the design securely in place so that the tracing does not become distorted, yet hold it lightly enough that the carbon does not smudge the material.

A Special Guide for Sewing Projects

Once you have the right amount of material on hand, you must then note your pattern-cutting instructions. Be sure that your material is pressed and wrinkle-free. Lay it out on a flat surface and very carefully fit whatever templates or pattern pieces you have to work with onto it in such a way that you get the maximum amount of cuttings from the fabric. At this point it might be necessary to juggle your pieces a little, for care taken now might very well make the difference between your having enough or not enough material with which to work. When you're ready to cut, take careful note of all your seam allowances. Cut out the pattern pieces with your good, sharp scissors and baste them together to be certain they are right. Then sew them together, either by hand or machine, with neat, even stitches and exactly the right color of thread.

For Crocheting and Knitting

In addition to everything we've mentioned above, there are still a few more special rules that apply to knitting and crocheting. The most important word to be aware of in both is *gauge*, which means the exact number of stitches you are getting to the inch with the needles or hook and the yarn and pattern stitch you are using. Working with anything short of the exact gauge will produce an ill-fitting garment, which in the end will prove to be a disaster to whatever effort you have put into your work. If you have more stitches to the inch than your instructions call for, then whatever you are making will be too small. Try a bigger hook or needles until you get the size that will give you the right number of stitches. If you are getting too few stitches, then your finished piece will be too large—and you should use a smaller hook or needles. Now, having established this much, relax and know that you are going to enjoy every minute of working on your project, for this is the only way your stitches will be smooth and even—unfortunately, personal uneasiness seems to reflect in the tension of work being done. When you are finished with the pieces, it is time to put your project together. Seaming crocheted or knitted pieces can be done in one of three ways. After being sure that the pieces are evenly matched one to the other, you can (1) sew them together on the wrong side of the work with a running backstitch taken about one stitch in from the edge; (2) weave them together, edge to edge, on the right side; (3) or put them together by working a row of single crochet stitches on the right side along each edge to be joined and then joining these crocheted edges together with a row of slip stitches, again on the right side of the work. Finally, all knitted and crocheted projects should be blocked for a perfect finish. This is done by pressing the project lightly with a warm iron over a damp cloth, keeping the iron in motion as you press so that it won't leave an impression on the piece when you are done. One last guideline: When crocheted edges are called for in any knitted or sewn pattern, be careful to see that you get the same number of stitches along each side so that your work lies flat and to work three stitches in each corner in order to ensure that the finished piece is correctly shaped.

Embroidery Work

For beautiful embroidery work, there are again a few special, but simple, guidelines, which, when followed, will make a great deal of difference in your work. First make sure that the needles you plan to use are sharp-pointed, of just medium length, and that they have long, slender eyes, which will help you to draw through multiple strands of thread when necessary without distorting the material or making holes in it as you embroider your stitches. Second, when several colors of thread are being used, work with several needles to avoid the abrasive wear and tear caused by having to rethread frequently.

Abbreviations Used in Knit and Crochet Projects

beg	beginning	pat	pattern
ch	chain	p	purl
CC	contrast color	rep	repeat
dec	decrease	rnd	round
dc	double crochet	sc	single crochet
hdc	half double crochet	sl st	slip stitch
inc	increase	sp (s)	space (s)
k	knit	st (s)	stitch (es)
lp (s)	loop (s)	tog	together
MC	main color	yo	yarn over

1

For Little People

Cuddly Crib Creatures

Made of soft, washable terry, these adorable little creatures, who rattle when you shake them, can be very welcome friends in a baby's crib. Either give them all together or make them one by one to suit the little one's fancy.

Materials

brown wrapping paper
1/3 yard terry, 36 inches wide, in each of blue, pink, and white; and small amounts of satin in blue, pink, and white
1 bag (1 pound) polyester stuffing
3 small rattles
felt scraps in black, white, and pink
1 skein embroidery floss in black
1½ yards satin ribbon, ⅝ inch wide, in pink
pipe cleaner

Elephant

Enlarge the pattern pieces on the brown wrapping paper and cut them out. Cut the blue terry and blue satin according to the pattern pieces, allowing ½ inch extra all around for a seam. Then, right sides together, sew the two parts of the body together, leaving a small opening for later stuffing. Right sides together, sew together the terry and satin pieces for each ear, leaving the straight edges open as indicated; then, again right sides together, sew the two pieces of each of the four legs together, leaving the top edges open. Turn all pieces right side out. Now firmly stuff the body and the legs, inserting a small rattle within the body stuffing, and sew up the openings on each of these five pieces. Sew the legs and ears in place. Then cut a piece of terry to measure ¾ inch X 4 inches for the tail, fold it in half lengthwise, seam the long and one short edge of the strip, turn the piece right side out, and sew the other short edge in place on the body. Cut the tusk out of white felt and the eye pieces out of the black and white felt. Sew on the eyes; then sew each pair of tusk pieces together, stuffing them lightly, and sew them in place. Next, embroider the mouth, eyelashes, and eyebrows with the black floss. Cut the heart out of pink felt, sew it in place as desired, and fancy her up with a perky pink satin bow tacked to the top of the head.

Little Pink Pig

Enlarge the pattern pieces on the brown wrapping paper and cut them out. Cut the pink terry and pink satin pattern pieces, following the pattern instructions and allowing ½ inch extra all around for a seam. Then sew and stuff the body, legs, and ears as for the elephant and sew them in place. For the tail, cut a piece of pink terry

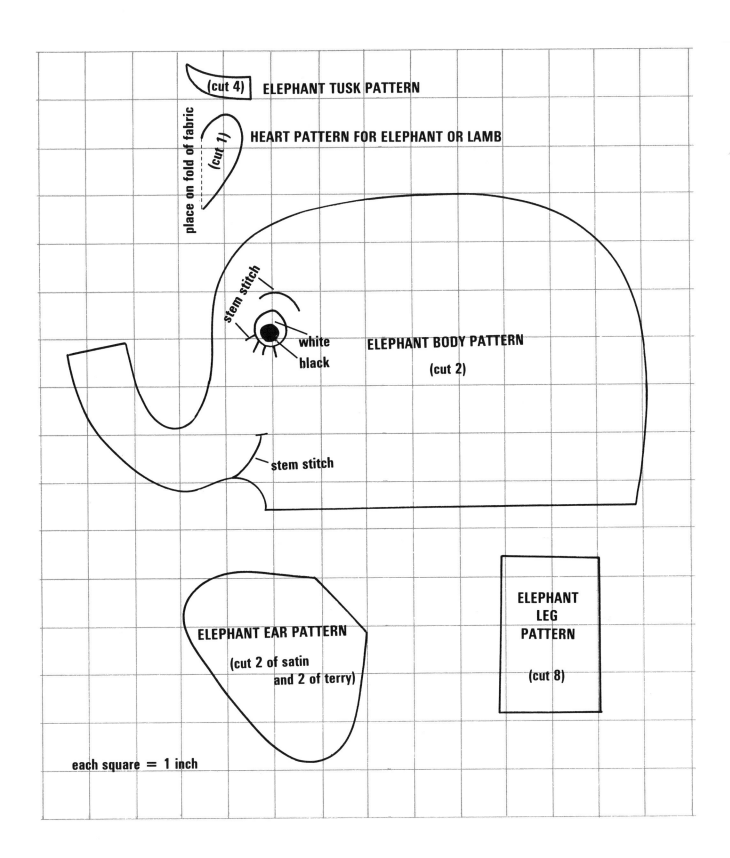

(cut 4)   ELEPHANT TUSK PATTERN

place on fold of fabric

(cut 1)   HEART PATTERN FOR ELEPHANT OR LAMB

stem stitch

white

black

ELEPHANT BODY PATTERN

(cut 2)

stem stitch

ELEPHANT EAR PATTERN

(cut 2 of satin
and 2 of terry)

ELEPHANT
LEG
PATTERN

(cut 8)

each square = 1 inch

13

to measure ¾ inch × 4 inches, sew it around a 4-inch length of pipe cleaner, twist it corkscrew style, and sew it on. Cut the eye pieces and nostrils from black and white felt and sew them in place. Finally, embroider the eyebrows and mouth as shown in the photograph and tie a pretty pink satin bow around the tummy.

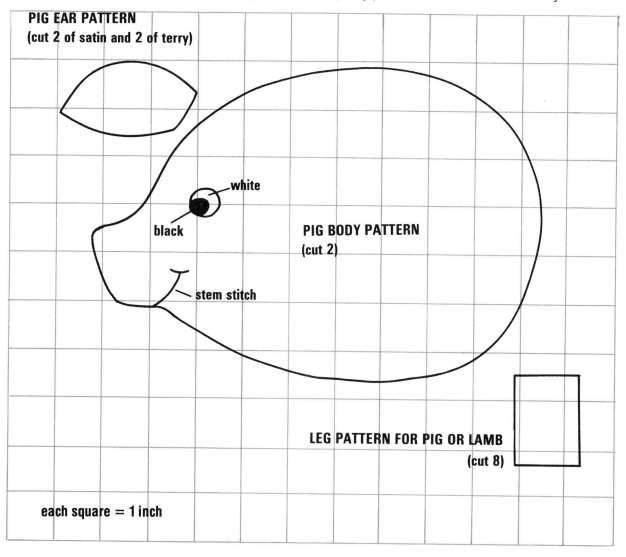

PIG EAR PATTERN
(cut 2 of satin and 2 of terry)

white

black

PIG BODY PATTERN
(cut 2)

stem stitch

LEG PATTERN FOR PIG OR LAMB
(cut 8)

each square = 1 inch

Lamb

Enlarge the pattern pieces on the brown wrapping paper and cut them out. Cut the white terry and white satin pieces, following the pattern instructions and allowing ½ inch extra all around for a seam. Then stuff the body, legs, and ears as for the other two creatures and sew them in place. Cut the tail piece from white terry and fold it in half, sew the two edges of it together, and sew it on the body. Finally, cut the eye pieces and the nose from the black and white felt, sew them on, and then embroider the eyebrows and mouth with the black floss. Finally, cut out a heart of pink felt, sew that on, and tie a pink satin bow around the neck.

14

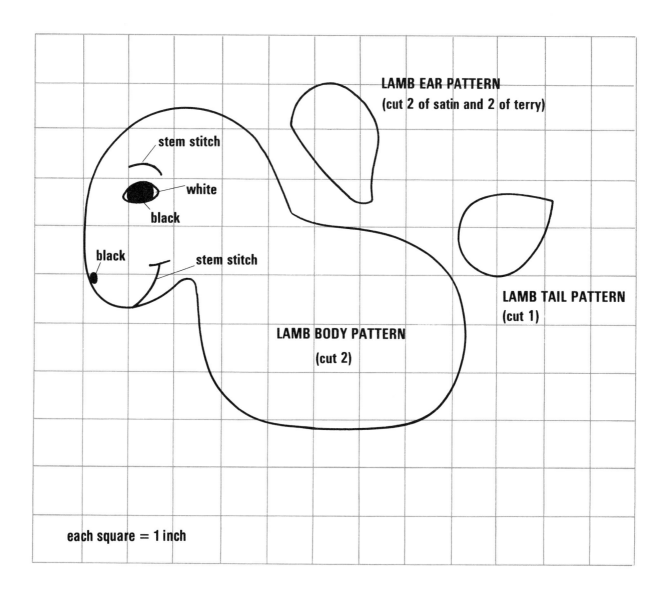

LAMB EAR PATTERN
(cut 2 of satin and 2 of terry)

stem stitch

white

black

black

stem stitch

LAMB BODY PATTERN
(cut 2)

LAMB TAIL PATTERN
(cut 1)

each square = 1 inch

A Warm and Cozy Patchwork Quilt

Measuring 28 inches x 36 inches, the baby's quilt shown here is patched in pink, white, and blue narrow-wale corduroy velvet so that it can be used for either a him or a her and thus be made long in advance of a baby's arrival. A three-dimensional look has been added by outlining the patches with crocheted trim (or braid if you prefer).

Materials

1⅛ yards narrow-wale corduroy, 45 inches wide, in blue, 1 yard in pink, and ½ yard in white
1¼ yards lining fabric, 36 inches wide, in pink or blue
1 crib-size package, 45 inches x 60 inches, polyester batting
6 ounces knitting worsted in blue or other desired color
aluminum crochet hook, size K

Quilt

Following the diagram, cut the colored patches as shown, adding ½ inch all around each patch for a seam allowance and being sure to cut on the grain line of the fabric as indicated. Right sides together, sew the patches together as shown on the diagram with a ½-inch seam. Cut a piece from the lining fabric that measures 31 inches × 39 inches. Right sides together and using a ½-inch seam, sew the completed patchwork piece to the lining along three sides, leaving one short end open; turn the piece right side out. Double the batting and cut a piece that measures 29 inches × 37 inches; insert the batting into the quilt. Next, turn under ½ inch of both pieces of fabric at the open edge and close the opening by hand. Then topstitch through all three layers along those lines indicated on the diagram. *Finishing:* Using double strands of yarn, crochet four lengths of chain that are long enough to outline the four corner pink patches, another long enough to outline the outer edge of the large center pink diamond and one more long enough to outline the inner edge and four long enough to outline each of the four mitered corners of the pink border edge. Sew them in place. (Instead of crocheting chain, you can substitute braid for this step if you wish.)

Note: **Diagram indicates measurement of 30 by 38 inches; after topstitching, quilt will measure 28 by 36 inches, as stated in directions.**

Color Key:

P = pink
B = blue
W = white

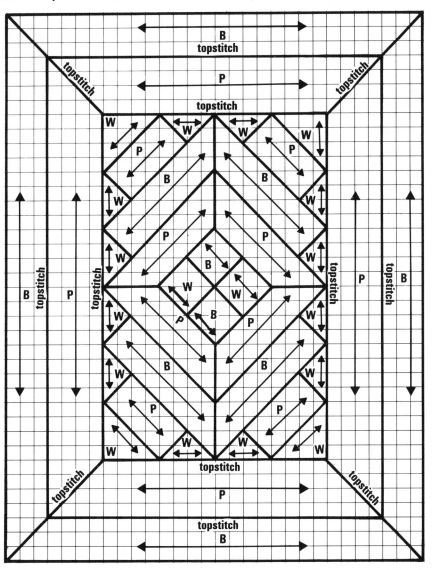

each square = 1 inch   **Arrows indicate grain of fabric**

17

A Winter-white Pram Suit

Fancied with pompoms and fringe, this four-piece set is knitted in the ever-popular seed stitch and made in an infant-to-six-month size with changes for one year given in parentheses.

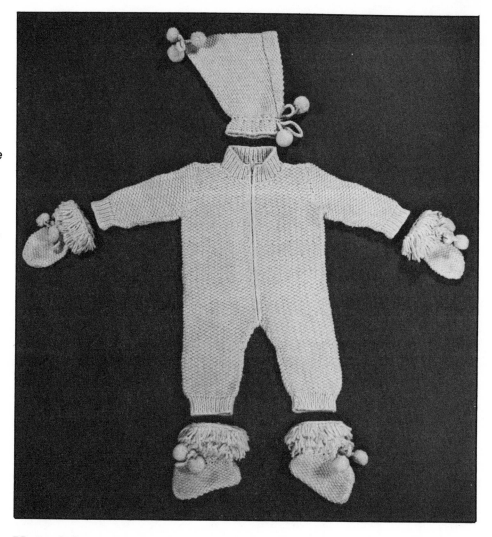

Materials

4 (5) skeins (4 ounces each) 4-ply knitting worsted in off-white
straight knitting needles, Nos. 7 and 10
aluminum crochet hook, size H
zipper, 13 (15) inches long, in off-white

Pattern Stitch: Row 1: *K 1, p 1, rep from * across the row, and end with k 1. Repeat this row for the pattern.

Gauge in Pattern Stitch: 9 stitches = 2 inches

Pram Suit

Left leg: With No. 7 needles, cast on 41 (47) sts and work in k 1, p 1 ribbing for 1½ (2) inches. Then change to No. 10 needles and pat st and work even for 4 (6) inches. Inc 1 st at beg and end of next row and every fourth row 3 times more—49 (55) sts—and then end with 1 row even. Place these sts on a holder. *Right leg:* Work as for left leg. After the last row has been completed, work for the body as follows: Work across the sts of the right leg and then across the sts of the left leg. Work even now in pat as established on 98 (110) sts for 9½ (11) inches. *Shape top:* Work across 23 (25) sts for the right front, join another ball of yarn, and bind off the next 4 (6) sts for one armhole; work across next 44 (48) sts for the back, join another ball of yarn, and bind off the next 4 (6) sts for the other armhole; work across next 23 (25) sts for the left front. Working each of the fronts together and the back separately now, dec 1 st at each armhole edge every fourth row twice. Then work even on both fronts until they measure 4 (4¾) inches above the start of the top shaping. On the next row, bind off 7 (8) sts at each neck edge of each front and then dec 1 st at each of these edges every other row 4 times. On each of the next 2 rows, bind off 4 (5) sts and then 6 (6) sts at each armhole edge for the shoulders. Finally, work the back portion even to the point of the shoulder bind-off. Bind off 4 (5) sts and then 6 (6) sts as on the fronts, and on the last row, bind off the remaining sts. *Sleeves:* With No. 7 needles, cast on 29 (33) sts and work in k 1, p 1 ribbing for 1½ (2) inches. Change to No. 10 needles and work even for 5 (6) inches. *Shape cap:* Bind off 2 (3) sts at beg of each of the next 2 rows and then dec 1 st at beg and end of every other row 9 (10) times; then bind off the remaining 7 (7) sts. *Finishing:* Sew shoulder, sleeve, and inside leg seams. With No. 7 needles and right side of work facing, pick up and k 56 (60) sts around the neck edge and work k 1, p 1 ribbing on these sts for 1¼ (1½) inches; bind off. Sew sleeves in place. Finally, work 1 row of sc around the center opening and sew the zipper in place.

Hat

With No. 10 needles, cast on 81 (85) sts and work even in pat st for 5 (6) inches. Then k 2 tog twice at beg and end of the next and every row until 5 sts remain, k 2 tog, k 1, k 2 tog, and bind off. *Finishing:* Fold pointed top section in half and sew the decreased edges together. With right side of work facing, pick up and k 47 (51) sts along the short straight edges of the hat. Then work a beading row as follows: k 2, *yo, k 2 tog, rep from * to last st, and end k 1. Finally, k 1 row, work even in pat st for 1½ inches, and bind off. For trim, crochet two chains with double strands of yarn, one 24 (26) inches long and the other 8 (10) inches. Draw the longer chain through the beading row for a tie, and trim each end of it with a pompom approximately 1½ inches in diameter. Tie the smaller chain into a bow, tack it in place ½ inch below the top point of the hat, trim each end with a pompom, and place one more pompom at the very top point of the hat, just above the bow. Finally, turn over the front center of the hat to make a 1½-inch cuff at its widest point, tapering it to a point on each side just above the beading row and tacking it in place.

Mittens

Make two: With No. 10 needles, cast on 27 (33) sts and work even in pat st for 2 (2½) inches. Then work a beading row as follows: *K 2 tog, yo, rep from * to last st, k 1. K 1 row now and then work even in pat for 2½ (2¾) inches more, placing a marker on the center st of the last row. Work a decrease row as follows: *K 1, k 2 tog, work in pat to within 2 sts before the marker, p 2 tog, sl marker, k 1, p 2 tog, in pat to within last 3 sts, k2. k1. Work the next 3 rows even. Now work another dec row as before, then 1 row even, rep these last 2 rows twice, bind off, and break off yarn, leaving a long thread. *Finishing:* Draw thread tightly through bound-off sts and sew side seam. With double strands of yarn, crochet a chain 14 (16) inches long and draw it through the beading row, attaching a small pompom to each end of the chain. Finally, cut some yarn into strands 3½ inches long. Knot two of them in every other st around the starting row of the mitten and then again around the row 1 inch below that top row.

Booties

Make two: Soles and sides: With No. 10 needles, cast on 23 (25) sts. Work even in pat for 4 inches and bind off. *Uppers:* Cast on 6 (8) sts and work in pat for 2 rows. Then inc 1 st at beg and end of next row, work 1 row even, rep these 2 rows, and then work even on 10 (12) sts until piece measures 2 inches from beg; bind off. *Finishing:* Fold sole and side pieces in half lengthwise and sew one short end on each piece together. Fit the rounded end of each upper into the joined piece and sew it in place. Then, with right side of work facing, pick up and k all sts around the two sides and the straight portion of the uppers. K 1 row, work a beading row as on the mittens, then work in pat for 2½ (3) inches, and bind off. Sew the back seam and, finally, make a chain as for the mittens, this one 14 (16) inches long. Draw it through the beading row, sew a small pompom to each end of the chain, and then fringe the top of the booties as the mittens.

Embroidered Crib Quilt with Bumpers and a Special Bib to Match

Embroidered with multicolored flowers, our quilt is further prettied with a ruffled eyelet edging and then made toasty warm with a washable polyester filler. The matching bumpers help to make the set a lovely dressing for any little one's crib. And the bib is just an extra touch. We used a pink-and-white-striped pillow ticking fabric with coordinated embroidery floss colors, but you can use any durable, washable fabric with colors of your choice.

Materials

2½ yards pillow ticking fabric, 36 inches wide, for the quilt, 2¼ yards for the bumpers, and ¼ yard for the bib, in pink and white stripes

9 skeins embroidery floss in pink and 4 skeins each in lilac, leaf green, and medium blue

1 crib-size package, 45 inches x 60 inches, polyester batting

6 yards eyelet edging, 2 inches wide, in white

4 pieces foam rubber, 2 inches thick x 7 inches wide, two of which are 48 inches long and two 26 inches long

brown wrapping paper

Quilt

Cut two pieces of the fabric, each 31 inches × 41 inches, and transfer on it the embroidery pattern. Then, following the diagram, embroider the multicolored flowers on one of the pieces. Turn under and press a ½-inch hem on all edges of each piece. Then double the batting, trim the double piece to measure 30 inches × 40 inches, and insert it between the two pieces of material. Now gather the eyelet with a needle and thread and insert it between the two layers of fabric along the outer edges, pinning it in place as you work. Sew all pieces together. With pink, embroider a French knot in the center of each of the embroidered flowers. Work these stitches through the top and bottom of the quilt and the batting and leave two long ends of the thread extending on the underside. Finally, tie these two strands together for a tufted effect—these will also hold the batting in place.

Color and Stitch Key:

Large flowers = lazy daisy stitch in pink
Flower center = French knots in pink
Vine = stem stitch in green
Vine tufts = stem stitch in blue or lilac

blue

lilac

QUILT EMBROIDERY PATTERN

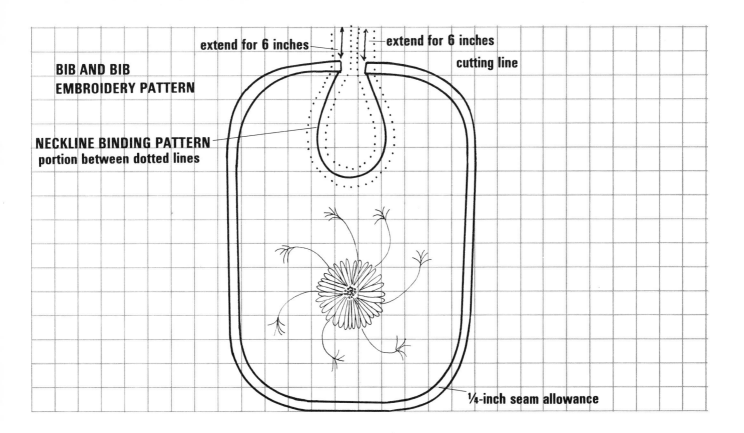

BIB AND BIB EMBROIDERY PATTERN

extend for 6 inches

extend for 6 inches

cutting line

NECKLINE BINDING PATTERN
portion between dotted lines

¼-inch seam allowance

Bumpers

Cut two pieces of fabric, each 17 inches × 76 inches, to cover the foam rubber and five strips, each 1 inch × 84 inches, for the bumper ties. Seam the two large pieces together across the short edges to make one long piece and then sew in a ½-inch seam on all four sides. Fold the piece in half widthwise and seam each of the short ends together, mitering the corners to fit over the ends of the foam. Mark three seamlines on the long strip that will run across its width, the first one 48 inches in from one end, the next one 26 inches in from the first, and the next 48 inches in from the last. Then on the right side of the work, sew through the two layers of material. For the ties, fold each of the 1-inch strips in half lengthwise. Press, fold each edge in half again so that the raw edges are inside, and press. Seam them along the open edges, and cut them into 12-inch lengths. Then sew five strips, spaced equidistantly, along both open edges of each of the 48-inch sections and three strips along both open edges of each of the 26-inch sections. Finally, fit the foam pieces into the sectioned-off bumper cover and tie each pair of the strips into a bow to keep the bottom edges of the cover closed, yet free to be removed for easy laundering. If a closer fit is desired, make a few tacking stitches between each set of ties.

Bib

On brown wrapping paper, enlarge the pattern for the bib, including the embroidery pattern, and cut it out. Cut two pieces of fabric, following the pattern, and transfer the embroidery pattern onto one. Cut one strip of fabric that is ⅞ inch × 62 inches long for the ruffle, piecing it as necessary, and another for the neckline binding and ties ¾ inch wide that follows the curve around the neckline and continues in one piece so that the strip extends 6 inches beyond the curve at each side of the neck. Work the embroidery on one bib piece as indicated on the pattern. Then turn under ⅛ inch along one long edge of the ruffle piece and topstitch it in place. Now gather the ruffle along the unfinished edge and pin it in place on the right side of the embroidered bib piece, pinning it right sides together so that the gathered edge of the ruffle is on the outer edge of the bib and the finished edge lies towards the center of the bib. Baste it in place. Lay the other bib piece on top, right sides together, and stitch around the outside edge ¼ inch in from that edge, leaving the neckline open. Turn the bib right side out. Turn under ⅛ inch on each edge of the neckline binding and topstitch in place, clipping the curves on the inner seam allowance as necessary so that the piece lies flat. Fold the finished neckline binding in half around the edge of the neckline opening and stitch it in place.

Left to right: *For Him, An Icelandic Cap and Scarf, p. 106;*
Pattern-knit Guitar Strap, p. 108; Tweedy Vest, p. 122; Book
Tote, p. 115.

A Robe of Calico and Crisp Crochet, p.50; Soft Furnishings for a Doll's One-bedroom Apartment, p.72.

Left and right: *Beachwear for Little Ones, p. 41*. Center:
Strawberries on Smocked Gingham, p. 33.

A Personalized Wall Hanging, p. 79 ; Silky, Tasseled Neckwear, p. 101.

Baby Carriers—One for Him and One for Her

Easy to make and comfortable to carry your son or daughter in from the time of their first outing up until they've grown quite a few months older, his is made of demin, trimmed with rickrack, and clearly labeled "My Son" while hers is in a flowered material and softly ruffled, as befits a very young lady.

Materials

brown wrapping paper
2 yards sturdy fabric of your choice, 45 inches wide
small amount of polyester batting
2 metal D rings, each 1½ inches wide and 2 inches high
2½ yards medium-width rickrack and 2 skeins embroidery floss in white for his; or 1½ yards
     pre-ruffled eyelet trimming, 1 inch wide, in white for hers

Carriers

Enlarge the pattern on brown wrapping paper, cut it out, and use it to cut two pieces from the fabric. Then cut one strip (A) 5 inches × 101 inches, piecing this strip as necessary, but leaving the center 10 inches seam-free, and one strip (B) 5 inches × 25 inches. From the batting, cut two pieces ¾ inch wide to follow the shape of the leg openings, one piece measuring 1½ inches × 19½ inches for strip B, and another 1½ inches × 28 inches for strip A. Turn under and press in place a ½-inch seam allowance on all four edges of both fabric strips and then fold each of them in half lengthwise; press. Place the two main pieces right sides together and sew the side seams and around the leg openings. Turn the piece right side out. Fit the leg-opening padding strips in place, pin them down, and then topstitch around them as shown on the pattern. Center the remaining padding strips into the appropriate fabric strips, and add the strips to the main piece as shown on the pattern, inserting the main piece into each strip to the fold of the strip. Topstitch the open edges of each strip, going through five layers of fabric in all, including the turnovers on the strip. Then topstitch around the three edges of each extended portion of each

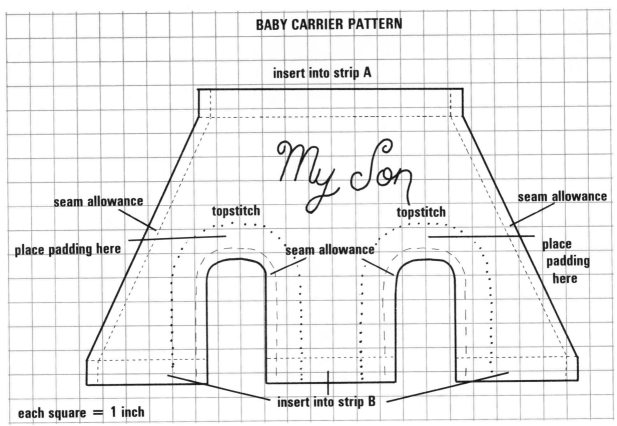

BABY CARRIER PATTERN

insert into strip A

My Son

seam allowance

topstitch

topstitch

seam allowance

place padding here

seam allowance

place padding here

insert into strip B

each square = 1 inch

strip. Fold each of the extensions of the two B strips in half around a metal ring and stitch them in place. *Finishing*: On his, with dressmaker's carbon, trace ''My Son'' as shown on the pattern. Then with triple strands of embroidery floss, chain-stitch the letters. Sew the rickrack around the topstitching on the leg openings and along the top and bottom edges of the center padded 10-inch portion of strip A. On hers, sew on five lengths of eyelet ruffle, one around the bottom of each leg opening and the remaining three in three adjacent rows across the back of the main piece just below the padded section of strip A. To wear the carrier, place baby's legs through the leg openings and hold him against the front of your body. Bring the straps over your shoulders, cross them in back, thread the ends through the D rings, and tie the ends behind your back.

New-fashioned Stroller Pants

Maybe there's really little new under the sun, but these stroller pants are certainly innovative. Just as warm as a blanket, a stroller pants set is, however, more comfortable for a baby because it eliminates the need for him to be bundled up. It is also much more convenient for mom because she can just slide baby into it—snowsuit and all. Since the suit slips over the stroller handles, mom doesn't need to worry about its slipping off either. These pants should fit any baby six to eighteen months old.

Materials

4 skeins (4 ounces each) bulky yarn in white, 3 skeins in rust, and 1 skein in charcoal
1 yard lining fabric, 45 inches wide, in white
1 crib-size package, 45 inches x 60 inches, polyester batting
straight knitting needles, No. 11
aluminum crochet hook, size K

Color and Stitch Pattern: Working all white and rust rows in reverse stockinette st and all charcoal rows in stockinette st, work in color pat as follows: 12 rows white, one stripe (3 rows charcoal, 2 rows rust, and 3 rows charcoal), 10 rows white, one stripe, 8 rows white, one stripe, 6 rows white, one stripe, 4 rows white, one stripe, and 4 rows white, working the last stripe and the last 4 rows of white on the back piece only.

Gauge in Stockinette and Reverse Stockinette Stitch: 2 stitches = 1 inch; 8 rows = 3 inches, using double yarn throughout.

Stroller Pants

Back: Starting at the bottom of the left leg and working in color and stitch pat throughout, cast on 9 sts and work even for 30 rows of the color pat. Place these sts on a holder. Work the right leg in the same manner, this time ending with the thirty-first row. Then cast on 4 sts at the end of this row for the crotch and work across the sts from the holder. Now continue working in pat on the 22 sts on the needle until completing the forty-seventh row of color pat. Then dec 1 st at beg and end of next row. Work even to the completion of the back, working the number of rows as indicated on the color and stitch pat at the beginning of the instructions; bind off. *Front:* Work as for the back except work the crotch on the thirty-fifth and thirty-sixth rows, work the dec at beg and end of fifty-third row above the start of the legs, and work the fewer number of stripes as indicated at the beginning of the instructions. *Inner leg and crotch gusset:* Working in reverse stockinette st with double strands of rust throughout, cast on 14 sts and work as follows: *Row 1:* Work even. *Row 2:* K first 3 sts tog, k across row. Rep Rows 1 and 2. Then work 1 row even, dec 1 st at beg of next row, and finally work even on 9 sts for 20 more inches. After this portion of the gusset has been completed, inc 5 sts to correspond to the decreases at the start of the piece and work them in the same manner, increasing now instead of decreasing. When there are 14 sts, work 1 row even and bind off. *Outside leg gussets (make two):* Working again with double strands of rust and the reverse stockinette st and starting at the bottom of the leg portion, cast on 14 sts, shape the piece as for the beginning of the crotch gusset, and when there are 9 sts, work even for 12 inches. Finally, dec 2 sts every other row 4 times, working these decreases on the opposite edge of those worked for the toe shaping; fasten off. Then make another gusset in the same manner, reversing the shaping. *Soles (make two):* With double strands of charcoal, cast on 9 sts and work even in reverse stockinette st for 5½ inches; bind off. *Finishing:* Block all pieces. Then, using them as pattern pieces, cut two matching pieces for each of these patterns, one from the lining material and one from the batting, adding a ¼-inch seam allowance on the lining material only. Now line the pieces on the wrong side of the work, first with a layer of the batting and then with a layer of the lining material. Turn the outer edge of the lining allowance under the batting and then sew the lining piece in place around the outer edge of each piece, tacking through the double layer of material and batting and leaving 1 st free at each edge of each knitted piece for seaming. With double strands of white, cast on 22 sts for additional lining of the upper portion of the back, work even in reverse stockinette st for 9½ inches, and bind off. Sew this additional knitted piece in place across the upper back and over the lining material. When all pieces have been lined, seam them together in the following way: Sew the inner leg and crotch gusset to the inner edge of the legs of the front piece, fitting the striped edges along the shaping of the toes and matching the crotch portions. Sew the two outer leg gussets in place, again fitting on the toe portions and stretching this gusset to reach to the top of the second-to-last white stripe on the front knitted piece. Join the back edges of the gussets to the knitted back piece, stretching the side gussets now to reach to the top of the third white stripe from the bottom. Sew on the soles. Next, with double strands of rust, crochet chains to fit along all the seamlines and around the top free portion of the front and back pieces. Sew these in place over the seams. Finally, crochet two 10-st chains with double strands of the rust at each corner of the back to slip over the stroller handles.

Strawberries on Smocked Gingham

The enchanting little black-and-white sundress shown here is smocked in cherry red and trimmed with three luscious strawberries. Made to fit a young lady between one and two years old, its length can be adjusted by opening any one or all of three invisible "grow" pleats that encircle the bottom of the skirt.

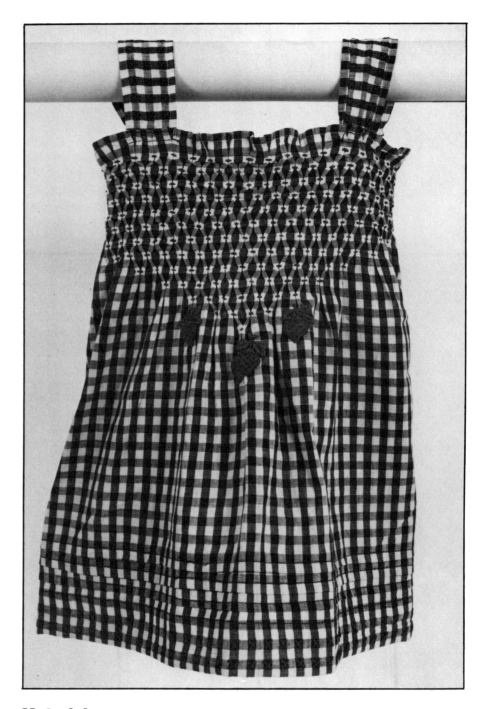

Materials

1 yard gingham, 36 inches wide, in ¼-inch-square black and white checks
6 skeins embroidery floss in cherry red
3 strawberry appliqués
zipper, 7 inches long, in black

Dress

Cut a 21-inch length out of the full width of the fabric, being sure to do this and all other cutting exactly on the edges of the squares. Then cut two strips for the straps, each 2¾ inches × 11½ inches, and two 2¾-inch × 17-inch strips for the ties on the back. Now fold over to the wrong side ¼ inch along the 36-inch width of the fabric, and then fold over another ¼ inch, in this way turning the raw edge of the fabric to the inside. Topstitch along this fold on the right side of the fabric one square down from the fold. *Smocking:* Using the full six strands of the embroidery floss, starting approximately 1 inch down from the top hemmed edge on a row of white squares at the fourth or fifth white square in from the left edge, working from top to bottom, and following the general smocking instructions given on the diagrams, work as follows: *Rows 1 and 3:* Work 35 smocking sts across. *Rows 2 and 4:* Work 33 sts across, starting and ending each row between the first and second sts of the previous row. *Row 5:* Skip 5 smocking sts and make the first smocking st on this row between the fifth and sixth sts on the row above, continue across, and end between the fifth and sixth sts from the other edge. Work 8 more smocking rows (including the sixth row, which is worked simultaneously with the fifth), starting and ending each new row now between the second and third sts of the previous row until 1 st remains. *Cross-stitch embroidery:* Working 2½ inches up from the bottom edge, embroider, again with six strands of the floss, one cross-stitch in each black square across the piece. Repeat this embroidery, stitch above stitch, on the next black row above the first row. On the shoulder straps, embroider a cross-stitch on the black square on each side of the center black row, working on every other row of black squares. *Finishing:* For the "grow" pleats, start the first row 4 rows up from the top row of cross-stitches along the bottom of the piece. Make this a ½-inch decorative pleat across the width of the material on the right side of the work, folding it downward and topstitching it in place on the right side. Then make two more pleats above this one in the same manner, spacing them ½ inch apart. Now fold the completed width of the material in half, right sides together, and stitch a center back seam, leaving a 7-inch opening at the top for a zipper. Insert the zipper. Finish the straps and ties by turning under ¼ inch along all long edges of each piece, then folding the raw edges to the inside another ¼ inch, and sewing these hems in place. Then hem the short edges and sew the straps on 1½ inches in from each side edge. Finally, hem the ends of the ties along the short edges, sew them in place at the top center back of the dress and tie them in a bow. Make a 2-inch hem at the bottom of the dress, and sew the three appliqués on below the smocking as shown in the photograph.

Smocking How-To

Work stitches in center of white squares only, from left to right.

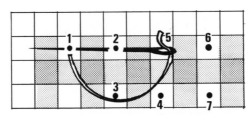

Bring thread up through square 1, make a small backstitch in center of square 2, make another small backstitch in center of square 1, and pull the thread to bring the two squares together.

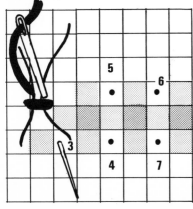

Insert needle down through fabric as shown and up into square 3. Keep material flat between sqaure 1 and square 3. Pull together 3 and 4 as for 1 and 2 and then insert needle down through square 4 and up into square 5, continuing across by working row above and then row below as established. Fasten off at end of completed two rows and start again at left edge.

Bib Tops—Pants for Him and a Skirt for Her

A colorful castle trims his top, and a rainbow and a pot of gold trim hers. The patterns for cutting the tops, pants, and skirt designed for sizes 3 and 4 are very simple.

Materials

Scraps of material in gold, medium blue, bright red, brown, and light and dark green for his bib; and medium blue, pink, aqua, turquoise, off-white, light and dark gold, and light and dark green for hers
fabric glue
embroidery floss in white
brown wrapping paper
½ yard fabric, 45 inches wide, in denim blue for each
9 inches elastic, ½ inch wide, for each
2 buttons, each ½ inch in diameter, in white for each
6 buttons, each 1 inch in diameter, in white for his

Bib Tops for Him or Her

Trace the patterns for the desired appliqué, cut them out, and use them to cut corresponding pieces, following the patterns for colors. From the medium blue, cut a square 5½ inches. Following the placement diagram, glue the pieces in place on the blue square, topstitch around each, and then embroider around each with the white floss and straight stitches. On brown wrapping paper, enlarge the pattern pieces for the bib and pants or skirt, cut them out, and use them to cut the number of pieces indicated on each pattern from the denim blue fabric. On one of the bib pieces, center and stitch the appliquéd square in place just below where the buttonholes are to go. Right sides together (appliquéd side in), seam the two bib pieces together

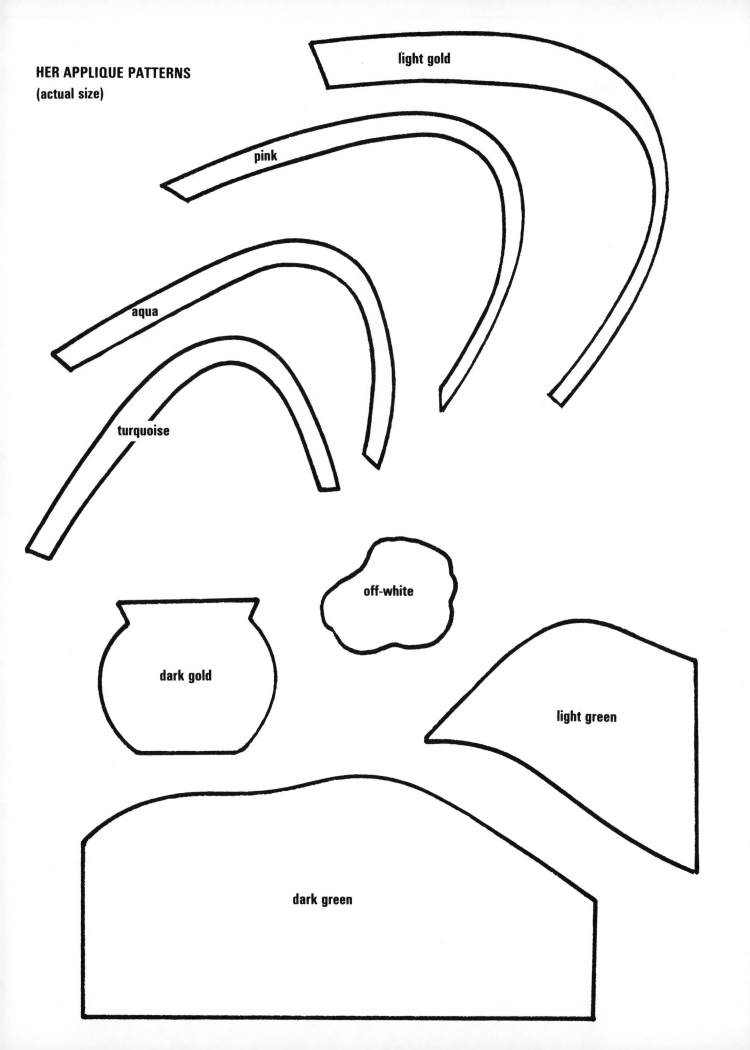

HER APPLIQUE PATTERNS
(actual size)

light gold

pink

aqua

turquoise

off-white

dark gold

light green

dark green

along three sides only, leaving one short edge (now the bottom edge) open. Turn right side out. Make the two buttonholes at the top edge where indicated on the pattern. Fold each strap in half the long way and turn the raw edges in ¾ inch; press in place and then topstitch. Fold the casing down on the skirt or pants back along the fold line, turn under the raw edge, and stitch, leaving the ends open. Draw the elastic through the casing and tack the ends in place. Right sides together, sew the side seams of the pants or skirt, and turn right side out. Right sides together, center the bib on the front portion of the bottom piece and seam the two pieces together, leaving the lining portion of the bib free. Turn the bottom raw edge of the lining piece under to cover the raw edges of the seam just made and hem in place. Turn under the remaining raw top edge of the front portion at each side of the bib and topstitch across the entire top edge of the skirt or pant front. Sew a ⅝-inch-wide hem at the bottom of the pants or skirt. Sew one small button to one end of each strap and the other end to the back bottom piece, placing each end 1 inch in from the side seam. Sew a row of three large buttons along each side seam of the pants, placing the first one about ¼ inch up from the bottom hem and the next two nearly touching each other. Finally, with the embroidery floss, embroider 2 rows of straight stitches just above the bottom hemlines of the pants or skirt.

PLACEMENT PATTERN FOR HER APPLIQUE (actual size)

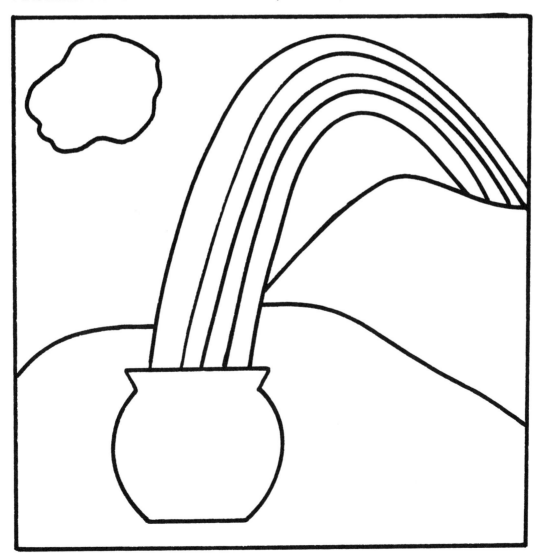

37

HIS APPLIQUE PATTERNS (actual size)

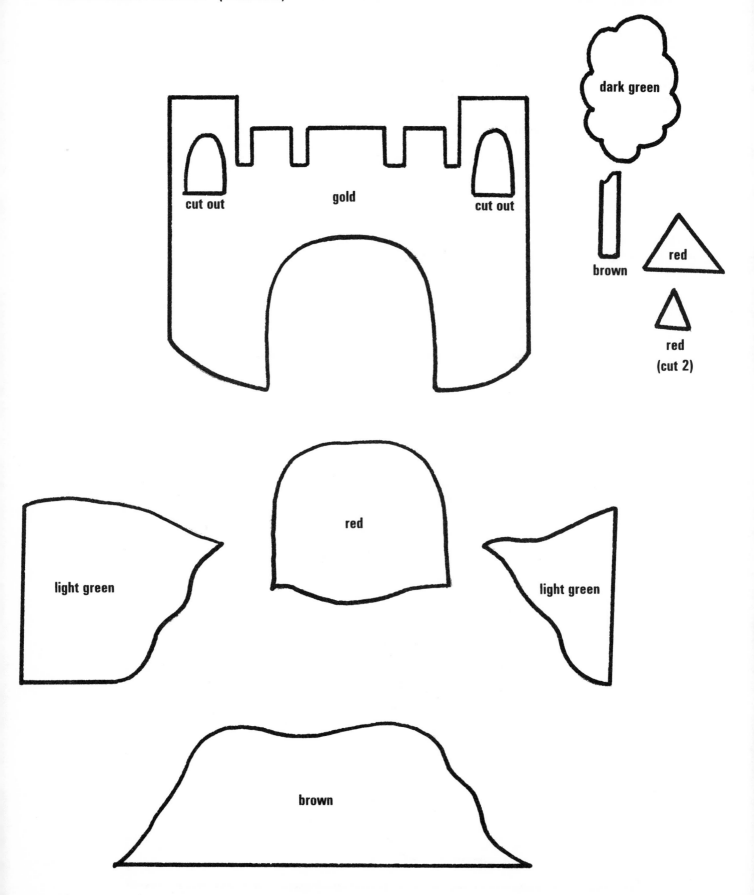

dark green

cut out

gold

cut out

brown

red

red
(cut 2)

light green

red

light green

brown

PLACEMENT PATTERN FOR HIS APPLIQUE   (actual size)

medium blue

red

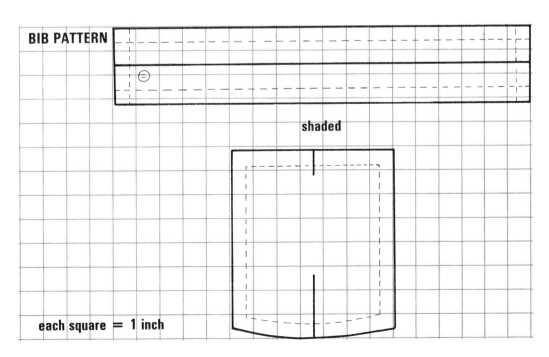

BIB PATTERN

shaded

each square = 1 inch

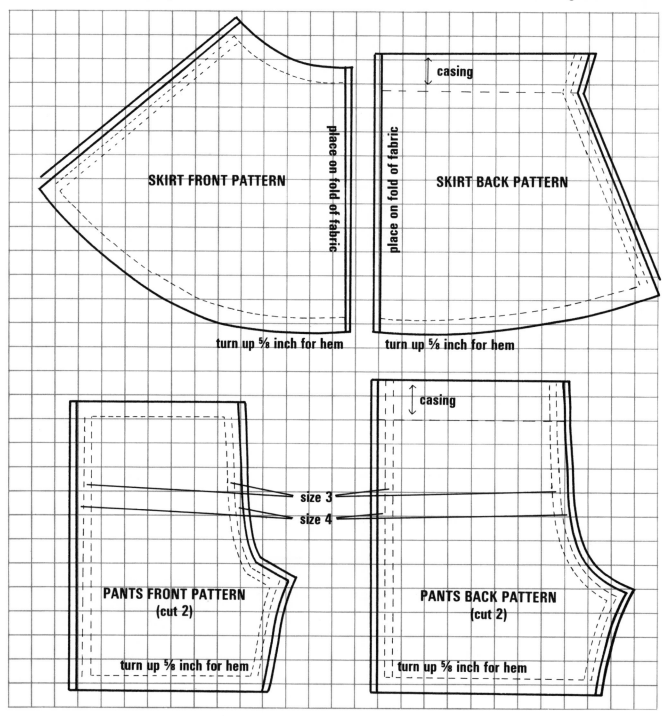

SKIRT FRONT PATTERN

place on fold of fabric

casing

place on fold of fabric

SKIRT BACK PATTERN

turn up ⅝ inch for hem

turn up ⅝ inch for hem

casing

size 3

size 4

PANTS FRONT PATTERN
(cut 2)

turn up ⅝ inch for hem

PANTS BACK PATTERN
(cut 2)

turn up ⅝ inch for hem

each square = 1 inch

Beachwear for Little Ones

Crocheted with double strands of a lightweight, mercerized crochet cotton, here is a smashing bikini plus a spare pair of clamdiggers for her, and for him, a pair of old-fashioned striped swim trunks. All pieces are designed for sizes 2, 3, and 4, with instructions for the larger sizes given in parentheses.

Materials

3 (4, 5) balls (150 yards each) lightweight, mercerized crochet cotton in white and 2 (3, 3) balls in red for his striped pants; 5 (6, 7) balls in white for her clamdiggers, 2 (3, 3) balls in white for her bikini top and bottom, and 3 balls in red for her three pieces

elastic, ¼ inch wide, in sufficient amount to fit around the waists of his trunks and her bikini bottom

elastic, 1¼ inches wide, in sufficient amount to fit around the waist of her clamdiggers

aluminum crochet hook, size E

Gauge in Single Crochet: 6 single crochet = 1 inch

His Striped Trunks

Starting at the top with red, working in sc with double strands of yarn throughout, and alternating 4 rows red with 4 rows white, ch 64 (67, 70). Then work even on 63 (66, 69) sts until piece measures 3 (3½, 4) inches. Inc 1 st now every ½ inch on one side only until there are 69 (72, 75) sts. *Leg shaping:* Dec 1 st at beg and end of every other row 8 times. Then work even on 53 (56, 59) sts for approximately 5 (5½, 6) inches more, ending with 4 rows of red. Fasten off, and make one more piece in the same manner, reversing the shaping. *Finishing:* Sew the two pieces together down the center back and front and along the inside leg seams. Make three lengths of ribbing as follows: With double strands of white, ch 7. Work in sc on 6 sts through the back lps only of the sts until one piece measures 18 (19, 20) inches for the waistband and each of the other two 7 (8, 9) inches for the leg bottoms; sew the ribbings onto the pants. Then make a casing at the waist: Attach a single strand of white yarn at the top of the center back of the ribbing, *ch 6, skip 1 inch, work a sl st at the bottom of the ribbing, ch 6, skip 1 inch, work a sl st at the top of the ribbing, rep from * around, and end the last sl st at either the top or the bottom, wherever it fits in. Cut a piece of elastic to fit the waist, draw it through, and securely sew together the short ends.

Her Clamdiggers

Using double strands of white, shape as for his striped trunks, ending hers 1½ inches earlier before the start of the leg shaping, working a 2-inch-wide ribbing at the top with the stitches of the casing spaced 1½ inches apart and using a 12-st chain between each st, and omitting the ribbing around the leg bottoms. *Finishing:* Draw elastic through the waistband casing and sew the short ends together. With double strands of red, make four chains, one to fit just under the ribbed waistband, another 2 inches below that, and the remaining two around the leg bottoms. Then on each of these, work a chain loop edging by *chaining 7, skipping 3 ch, working a sl st in the next ch, and repeating from * across the row. Sew each of these strips in place and then tack down the center of each loop so that it stays flat.

Her Bikini Bottom

Back: Starting at the crotch with double strands of white, ch 15 (17, 19) sts. Then work even in sc on 14 (16, 18) sts for 6 rows, inc 1 st at beg and end of every other row 14 times and then every row 10 times. Work even on 62 (64, 66) sts for 13 rows and fasten off. *Front:* Ch as for the back and then, after the first row of sc, inc 1 st at beg and end of every other row until there are 40 (42, 44) sts. Work even across the next row, ch 12, and turn. On the next row, work across 11 sts of the chain and across the center 40 (42, 44) sts, ch 12, and turn. Now work on 62 (64, 66) sts for 13 rows and fasten off. *Finishing:* Sew side seams. Make a top ribbing and casing as for the boy's striped trunks, sew it in place, and draw the narrow elastic through. With double strands of white, work 54 (56, 58) sc around each leg opening. Finally, with double strands of red, make three chain loop edgings as for the clamdiggers, one to fit around each leg opening and the other around the top just below the ribbing: sew these in place.

Her Bikini Top

Make two: With double strands of white, ch 16 (18, 20) and work 6 rows of sc on 15 (17, 19) sts. Then dec 1 st at beg and end of every row 7 times and fasten off. *Finishing:* With double strands of white, work 1 row of sc around each piece. Then with double strands of red, work chain loop edgings long enough to trim around each piece and sew them on. Finally, space the two top pieces ¾ inch apart and join them with two double-strand red chains, one going from the inside lower left corner to the inside lower right corner and the other from the inside upper right corner to the inside upper left corner. Now work a chain diagonally from the upper right corner to the lower left and from the upper left to the lower right, forming an X in the center between pieces. Next, with double strands of red, make one ch-5 loop at the outside bottom corner of both the right and left portions of the joined top. With four strands of red, crochet two chains, each approximately 22 inches long, and attach one to the center top point of each piece. To tie them, cross the chains behind the neck, draw each chain through the corresponding side loop, and tie the two together in the back.

Rainbow-trimmed Playsuit and Espadrilles for a Sophisticated Toddler

Very brightly striped rainbow trim on this black yoga-styled suit helps make this outfit a very special one. Instructions are written for a twelve-month size, with changes for an eighteen-month-old given in parentheses. Young, diaper-wrapped sophisticates will already be old enough to sense how great they look in it, while mommie will be very proud of having crocheted and put it all together in practically no time at all. And with the little red wrap-around-the-ankle espadrilles added to this spectacular though very practical set—well!

Materials

3 (4) skeins 4-ply knitting worsted (4 ounces each) in black (MC) and 2 ounces each in red (A), yellow (B), blue (C), and green (D), and 2 additional ounces in red (A) for the espadrilles aluminum crochet hooks, sizes G and I

Pattern Stitch: Row 1: *Sc in the second ch from hook, dc in the next, rep from * across the row, and end with 1 sc in the last ch, ch 2, and turn. *Row 2:* *Dc in the first st, sc in the next, rep from * across the row, end with 1 dc, ch 1, and turn. *Row 3:* Work 1 sc in each dc and 1 dc in each sc of the previous row. Repeat Row 3 for the pattern, always chaining 1 st to turn when the first st is a sc and 2 sts when it's a dc.

Gauge in Pattern Stitch: 4 stitches = 1 inch on size G hook; 5 stitches = 2 inches on size I hook.

Pants

Left leg: Starting at the bottom with MC and size I hook, ch 32 (34). Work in pat on 31 (33) sts for 2 rows and then break off MC. Working in sc, work a multicolored stripe of 2 rows A, 2 rows B, 2 rows C, and 2 rows D. Then, work in MC pat st again

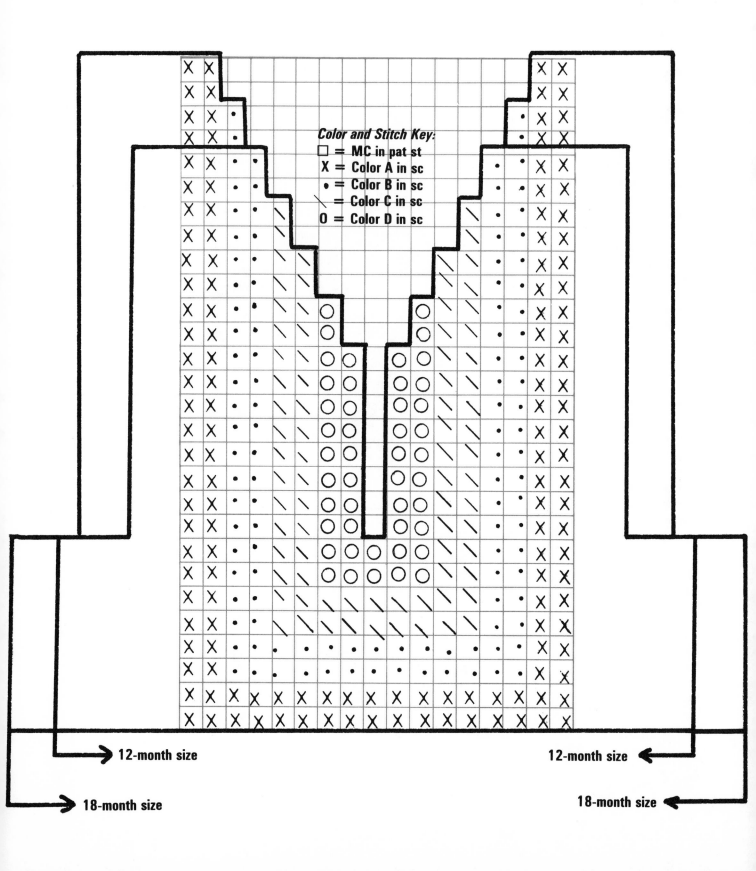

Color and Stitch Key:
☐ = MC in pat st
X = Color A in sc
• = Color B in sc
╱ = Color C in sc
O = Color D in sc

12-month size

12-month size

18-month size

18-month size

until piece measures 8 (9) inches, or the desired length to the crotch, ending with a wrong-side row. Continuing in MC pat st, dec 1 st at beg of row and then work across remaining 29 (31) sts. Start the center bottom of crotch. On next row, dec 1 st at beg of row and then work across remaining sts. Then work 1 row even. Rep these last 2 rows twice and then work even on remaining 27 (29) sts until piece measures 7½ (8½) inches or desired length above the start of the crotch. Fasten off. *Right leg:* Work to correspond to the left leg, reversing the shaping. *Finishing:* Sew the inner seams of each leg. Sew front and back crotch seams. Now work 2 rows of MC sc around the top of the pants, working 1 st in each st around. Fasten off. Finally, with MC, make a chain of 36 (40) sts for a drawstring tie around the waist, weave it through the row of spaces between the last 2 rows of sc, and knot each end of the chain.

Top

Back: Starting at the bottom with MC and size I hook, ch 28 (32). Work in pat on 27 (31) sts until piece measures 8 (9) inches or desired length to underarm, ending with a wrong-side row. *Shape armholes:* On the next row, sl st across 3 sts, work in pat to within the last 3 sts, ch, and turn. Work even now on 21 (25) sts for 4½ (5½) inches, ending with the wrong-side row. *Shape shoulders:* Work in pat across the first 6 sts and fasten off. Then skip the center 9 (13) sts for the back of neck, attach yarn again, and work in the same manner across the remaining 6 sts for the other shoulder. *Front:* Work as for the back until piece measures 5½ (6½) inches. Then follow chart to completion for the shaping and color design for the top of this piece. *Sleeves:* Starting at bottom with MC, ch 26 (28). Work in pat on 25 (27) sts for 2 rows and then work the multicolored stripe on these sts in the same way that the stripe was worked at the bottom of the pants. When completed, work even in MC pat st until piece measures 8 (9) inches or desired length from start. Fasten off. *Finishing:* Sew side and shoulder seams. Sew sleeve seams from the bottom to within 1½ inches of the top. Sew sleeves in position, fitting the open top portions of the sleeves into the armholes. With MC, work 1 rnd of sc around the opening in the front of the yoke and around the neck edge. Then work 1 row around the neck edge only, working this last row as follows: *1 sc in first st, ch 1, skip 1 st, 1 sc in next st, ch 3, sl st in first ch of the ch-3 just made, skip 1 st, rep from * around, and end with 1 sc in last st at the other end of neck. Fasten off. Then, with MC make a chain in the same manner as the drawstring for the pants and draw it through the ch-1 spaces around the top of the neck.

Espadrilles

Make two: Soles: With A and size G hook, ch 6 (8). Work 1 sc in second ch from hook and 1 sc in each of the next 4 (6) ch, ch 1, and turn. Working in sc throughout, work 1 row even and then inc 1 st at beg and end of next row. Work even on 7 (9) sts for 10 (12) rows. Dec 1 st at beg and end of the next row and, without fastening off, work 1 rnd of sc around the entire piece, rounding out the corners. Continuing around, work another rnd of sc, working this one through the back lps of the sts only. Finally, work 2 more rnds of sc through both lps. Fasten off. *Front uppers:* Mark the center 5 (7) sts at one short end of the piece for the front of the espadrille. Then attach the yarn in the first of these 5 (7) sts, work across them in sc, and join the end of this row with a sl st to the top st at the other side of the espadrille, ch 1, and turn. Now work another row of sc, increasing 1 st at beg and end of this row and again joining the last st with a sl st to the nearest st at the top of the espadrille. Work 3 rows even on 7 (9) sts, each time joining with a sl st. Fasten off. *Cross bands (make two):* Ch 10 (12) and fasten off. Sew one end of each to each front corner of the shoe, cross them, and sew the other ends to the side edges of the shoes just in front of the ankle, at the same time tacking down the first st worked on the last row of the front upper. *Ankle tie:* Ch 50 (60), work 4 sc into center 4 sts at the top of the back of the espadrille, ch 50 (60) more, and fasten off. Knot ends of the tie.

Nursery-Rhyme Characters on a Flying Mobile

Familiar friends for little people—Mary; Mary, Quite Contrary, Little Miss Muffet, Jack-Be-Nimble, and Peter, Peter, Pumpkin-Eater—are all joined together in a mobile designed for the pure pleasure of watching them swing and sway with the slightest breeze. Easily made of felt, they're completely detailed with the spider, the pumpkin, the candlestick, and all the other items related to them in nursery-rhyme books.

Materials

brown wrapping paper
¼ yard felt, 72 inches wide, in each of peach, light blue, and white
felt scraps in black, orange, and red
small amount knitting worsted in black
1 skein embroidery floss in each of black, orange, and green
2 yards grosgrain ribbon, ⅝ inch wide, in orange
steel crochet hook, #10
1 yard lightweight wire
small amount of polyester stuffing
dowel stick or other rod, 14 inches long, in white
white glue

Little Miss Muffet

On the brown wrapping paper, trace patterns A through E and cut them out. Then cut out the felt pieces, again following the pattern instructions for color and other specifics. Sew the two body pieces together with an overcast stitch on the right

46

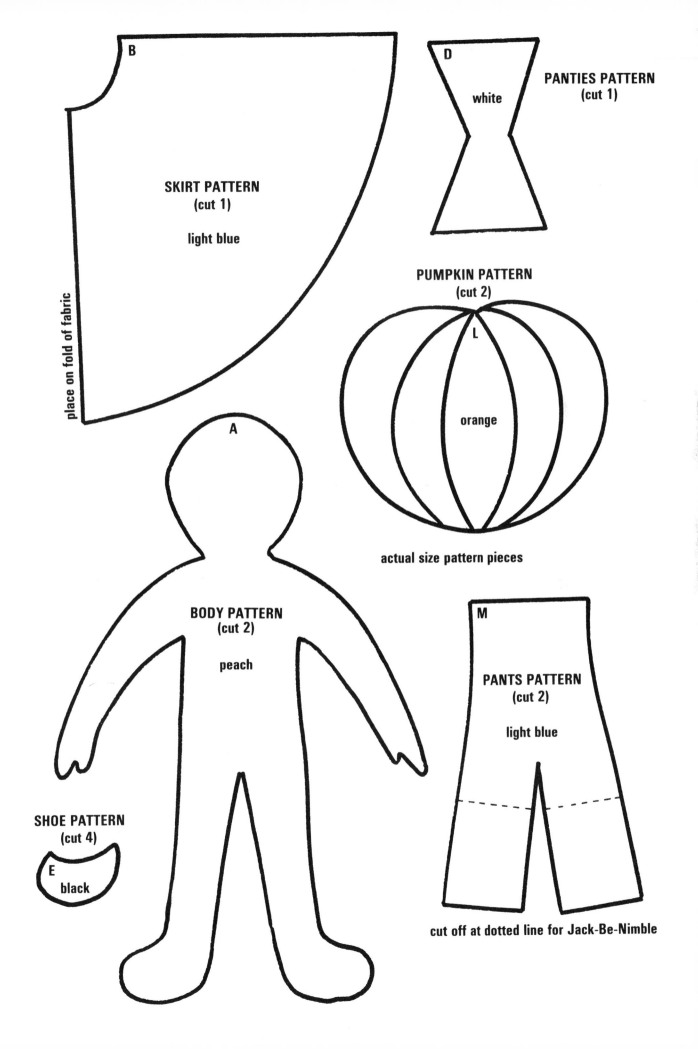

SKIRT PATTERN
(cut 1)

light blue

place on fold of fabric

B

PANTIES PATTERN
(cut 1)

D

white

PUMPKIN PATTERN
(cut 2)

L

orange

actual size pattern pieces

A

BODY PATTERN
(cut 2)

peach

PANTS PATTERN
(cut 2)

M

light blue

cut off at dotted line for Jack-Be-Nimble

SHOE PATTERN
(cut 4)

E

black

side of the work, stuffing the inside firmly as you stitch. Fit the blouse onto the body and sew the side and underarm seams, fit on the panties and sew the side seams, and then wrap the skirt around the body, placing the opening in the center back and then seaming the opening. Sew two shoe pieces to each foot. Tack the forearms to the upper arms at the elbows so that the arms are in an upright position, as shown. *Hair:* Cut black yarn into 4-inch-long strands, lay them side by side over the head, and glue them in place. *Bonnet:* Cut a 2¾-inch-diameter disk from light blue felt. With needle and thread, gather it around the edge to fit Miss Muffet's head and then tack it in place. Embroider two around black eyes and use a piece of red felt to make an "O" for a surprised mouth, gluing it in place. Finally, for the spider, cut a ½-inch-diameter disk from black felt. With the yarn, crochet six 1½-inch-long chains for legs. Tack the pieces onto the skirt as shown in the photograph.

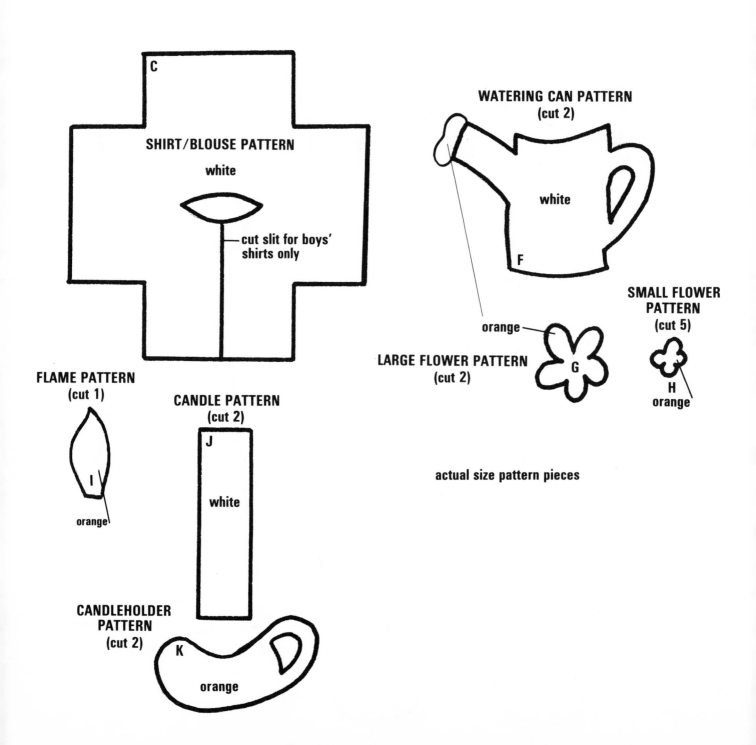

SHIRT/BLOUSE PATTERN

white

— cut slit for boys' shirts only

C

WATERING CAN PATTERN
(cut 2)

white

F

SMALL FLOWER PATTERN
(cut 5)

orange

H

LARGE FLOWER PATTERN
(cut 2)

orange

G

actual size pattern pieces

FLAME PATTERN
(cut 1)

orange

I

CANDLE PATTERN
(cut 2)

J

white

CANDLEHOLDER PATTERN
(cut 2)

K

orange

Mary, Mary, Quite Contrary

Using pattern pieces A through H, make body and clothing as you did for Miss Muffet and add the hair in the same way except use 8-inch-long yarn strands and ½-inch-long pieces for the bangs. Sew together the two watering-can pieces, stuffing them lightly, and tack the can to one hand. Embroider two round black eyes and use a bit of red felt glued to the face for a mouth. Finally, glue a large flower to the skirt and one to the watering can. Pierce each of the small flowers with a 2½-inch-length of wire, fix each in place with a drop of glue, twist the wires together to form a bouquet, wrap her hand around it, and tack the hand in place.

Jack-Be-Nimble

Using pattern pieces A, C, E, I, J, K, and M, complete the body and clothing in the same way as for Miss Muffet. Add the hair in the same way except trim it to be a little shorter than the others. Add the same facial features. Then stitch together each of the three pairs of pieces for the candlestick, leaving the tops of the holder and the candle open. Insert the flame into the candle opening and tack it in place. Insert the candle into the holder opening and tack it in place. Insert one of Jack's hands through the handle of the holder.

Peter, Peter, Pumpkin-Eater

Using pattern pieces A, C, E, L, and M, follow the earlier instructions for completing the body, clothing, and facial features; make the hair as for Jack's. Stitch together the two pumpkin pieces, stuffing them lightly as you sew. Embroider the markings with orange floss, and twist and sew to the top of it a tripled 1-inch length of green floss. Finally, leaving Peter's arms down, tack the pumpkin in place in Peter's hands.

Finishing: To complete the mobile, cut two pieces of ribbon, each 8 inches long, and two, 11 inches long. Arranging the characters as we have or as you desire, tack the back of each head to the end of a ribbon and sew the other end of the ribbon around the dowel. Then cut a piece of ribbon 26 inches long and stitch each end around one end of the dowel in proper position for hanging.

A Robe of Calico and Crisp Crochet

Our easy-to-make blue calico robe becomes something quite special when edged with crisp white crochet and given a pure white crocheted yoke ornamented with a little calico butterfly perched up near one shoulder. Instructions are written for a small size (8–10), with changes for medium (12–14) and large (16–18) given in parentheses. Incidentally, the medium size will fit a small-size woman and the large will fit a medium.

Materials

2 yards calico, 54 inches wide, in a blue print
3 (3, 4) balls (250 yards each) lightweight crochet cotton in white
steel crochet hook, No. 4
brown wrapping paper
zipper, 23 inches long, in blue
1 skein embroidery floss in white

Crochet Edging Pattern: Row 1: Ch 1, 1 sc in second ch from hook, 1 sc in each of next 2 ch, *ch 4, 1 sc in fourth ch from hook (picot made), 1 sc in each of next 2 ch, ch 9, turn, skip (2 sc, 1 picot, and 2 sc just made), 1 sc in next sc, turn, 11 sc in ch-9 sp, 1 sc in each of next 5 ch of foundation chain, rep from * across, and end last repeat with 11 sc in the last ch-9 sp; fasten off.

Gauge in Single Crochet: 8 stitches = 1 inch; 10 rows = 1 inch.

Robe

Cut one piece of fabric for the skirt that measures 39 inches (or the desired length from just below the bust line to the bottom) × 48 (51, 54) inches. For the sleeves, enlarge the pattern on brown wrapping paper, cut it out, and use it to cut two. Lay all pieces aside and, working in single crochet throughout, make the yoke as follows: *Right front:* Ch 61 (67, 73) and then work on 60 (66, 72) sts for 1¼ (1½, 1¾) inches. To shape armhole, sl st across 6 sts and work on remaining 54 (60, 66) sts until yoke measures 8½ (9, 9½) inches in all from start, ending at neck edge. To shape neck and shoulders, dec 1 st at neck edge every other row 12 times and, at the same time, dec 6 sts at side edge (shoulder dec) after the seventh (sixth, fifth) neck dec has been made. Then, continuing to shape neck, rep the shoulder dec on every other row until 6 sts remain. Fasten off. *Left front:* Work to correspond to right front, reversing all shaping. *Back:* Ch 121 (133, 145) and work even on 120 (132, 144) sts until piece measures 1¼ (1½, 1¾) inches. To shape armholes, sl st across 6 sts at beg of the next row, work to within the last 6 sts, ch, and turn. Work even now on 108 (120, 132) sts until piece measures same length as front to the start of the shoulder shaping. Shape shoulders (now on both side edges) in the same manner as the shoulder was shaped on each of the fronts and after the fifth (sixth, seventh) shoulder decreases have been made, shape neck: Work to within the center 12 sts, ch 1, and turn. Working on these sts only, dec 6 sts at each end of every other row until 6 sts remain. Fasten off. Return to row where neck shaping began, skip center 12 sts, and work the other side of the back to correspond. *Finishing:* Hem both sleeve bottoms and one of the 48 (51, 54)-inch robe edges. Insert the zipper between the two short edges, setting the top of it at the unhemmed longer edge. Hem both edges of the portion remaining open below the zipper and then sew the two edges together for 2 inches, leaving the remaining portion open. Seam the crocheted yoke at the shoulders and side seams. Sew the yoke to the top of the skirt portion, evenly gathering the material of the skirt to fit into the yoke. Sew the sleeve seams and then sew the sleeves in place. Make strips of edging long enough to fit around the entire yoke and two additional 11-inch-long strips to fit around the sleeve bottoms, as shown. Sew the edging in place. Sew on a hook and eye at the top of the zipper if desired. Finally, trace and cut out the butterfly pattern; use it to cut a calico butterfly. Embroider it according to the pattern and sew it to the left portion of the yoke, as shown in the photograph, stuffing it lightly if desired and turning under seam allowance, clipping curves as necessary.

BUTTERFLY PATTERN (actual size)

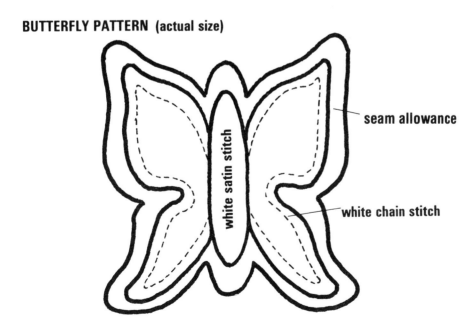

seam allowance

white satin stitch

white chain stitch

Andy, A Favorite Pet

Although Andy is neither a pure breed nor even a real dog, he does shape up into the kind of sweet creature that can be cuddled. Measuring 24 inches in length—practically life-size—Andy is made of a soft, plushy material and can be put together in just a few hours.

Materials

brown wrapping paper
3 yards soft, plush fabric, 36 inches wide, in brown
2 bags (1 pound each) polyester stuffing
velvet scrap in black
felt scraps in red, white, black, and tan
fabric glue
1¼ feet braid, 2 inches wide, in red
1 metal buckle, 1¾ inches x 2 inches, and a narrow metal chain, 5 inches long, in gold
small amount of embroidery floss in brown
5 inches narrow cord in brown
cardboard

Left to right: *For Cold Weather, A Thick, Crocheted Poncho for Him or Her, p. 132; New-fashioned Stroller Pants, p. 31; Granny-square Cap and Scarf Set, p. 102; Quilted Calico Carryall, p. 117.*

Satin Stardust mobile, p. 66; Cuddly Crib Creatures, p. 12; A Warm and Cozy Patchwork Quilt, p. 16; A Big, Friendly, Happy Polar Bear Rug, p. 59.

Cat and Mouse Games, p. 64; Bib Tops—Pants for Him and a Skirt for Her, p. 35.

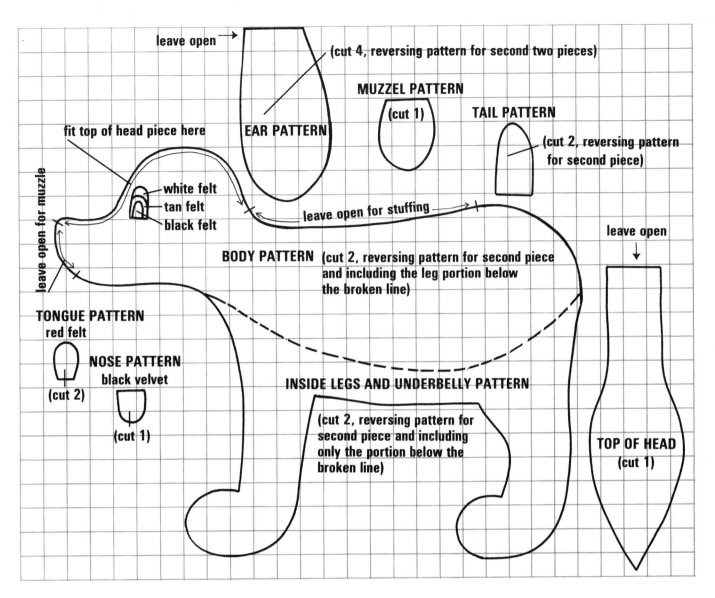

leave open →

(cut 4, reversing pattern for second two pieces)

MUZZEL PATTERN

(cut 1)

TAIL PATTERN

EAR PATTERN

(cut 2, reversing pattern for second piece)

fit top of head piece here

leave open for muzzle

white felt
tan felt
black felt

leave open for stuffing

leave open
↓

BODY PATTERN (cut 2, reversing pattern for second piece and including the leg portion below the broken line)

TONGUE PATTERN
red felt

NOSE PATTERN
black velvet

INSIDE LEGS AND UNDERBELLY PATTERN

(cut 2)

(cut 1)

(cut 2, reversing pattern for second piece and including only the portion below the broken line)

TOP OF HEAD
(cut 1)

each square = 1 inch

Andy

Body: On brown wrapping paper, enlarge or trace all the pattern pieces, according to the pattern instructions, and cut them out. Being sure each time that the plush side of the pieces, when cut, will be on the outside of the dog (the pattern must be reserved for each piece needing to be cut twice—body, legs, ears, etc.), cut out the plush pieces, the tongue and eye pieces from the colors of felt indicated on the patterns, and the nose from the black velvet. Making ¼-inch seams on the wrong side of the work, sew the two pieces for each ear and the two tail pieces together, leaving an opening at the top of each; turn right side out. Sew the two inside leg pieces, right sides together, to the corresponding body pieces, and sew the center seam of the body between the two inner leg pieces to make the underbelly. Right sides together, sew the back and under-chin seams to the points indicated on the pattern and then fit the muzzle in place at the front of the face; sew it on. Position the top of the head so that the straight edge meets the muzzle and the pointed end meets the back seam and, right sides together, sew it on. Now turn the piece right side out, stuff the body firmly, and close the back opening. Stuff the tail and sew it in place; sew on the ears, turning as you sew the raw edges at the top of each to the inside. *Facial features:* Sew the nose in place, stuffing it lightly as you go. Sew together the two red felt tongue pieces, placing a small amount of stuffing between the pieces, and then sew the completed piece in place. Glue the three eye pieces together to make each of the eyes, following the pattern instructions, and glue the completed pieces in place. Then, from the velvet, cut five ⅜-inch-wide strips: two that are 2 inches long for the eyebrows, two that are 2½ inches long for the upper part of the mouth, and one that is 1¾ inches long for the under part. Curving the eyebrows into arches, the two upper pieces of the mouth into a smile, and the under part of the mouth below the tongue, glue on the pieces.

Finishing: Thread the strip of red braid through the buckle, hemming the ends, and tack it around the neck for a collar. For the nametag, cut two 1¼-inch-diameter disks from the white felt and one from the cardboard. Embroider with brown floss the desired name on one of the felt disks; then glue the two felt pieces together with the cardboard between. Edge the finished piece by gluing on the strip of narrow brown cord. Finally, attach the disk to the center of the gold chain and sew the two ends of the chain to the bottom of the collar.

A Big, Friendly, Happy Polar Bear Rug

The expressive polar bear rug shown here is made of a soft, white, fake fur. It could be a charming accessory in a young baby's nursery, as well as a friendly and familiar pet for the baby when he grows up a bit.

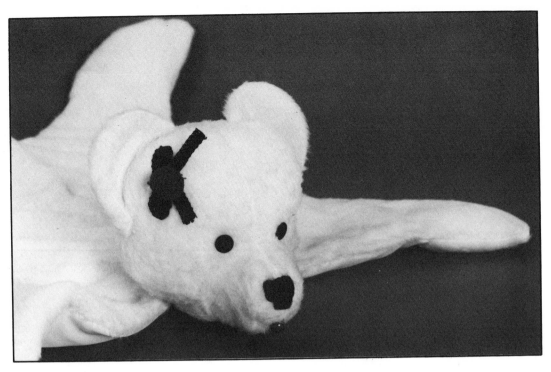

Materials

brown wrapping paper
1½ yards fake fur, 45 inches wide, in white
¾ yard satin lining fabric, 36 inches wide, in white
1 bag (1 pound) polyester stuffing
1 crib-size package, 45 inches x 60 inches, polyester batting
small amount medium-weight yarn in black
large-eyed embroidery needle
3 small shank buttons, two in black and one in red
small pompom in red
small piece of ribbon in black

Rug

On the brown wrapping paper, enlarge the pattern pieces and cut them out. Fold the fake fur in half, right sides together, and cut the main body piece plus two underside front paw pieces and one underside tail-end piece, following the pattern instructions and adding ½ inch all around for a seam allowance. Still cutting through double thicknesses, cut the head, nose, and ear pieces, this time adding no seam alllowance. From the lining fabric, cut a piece for the underside as indicated on the pattern, adding a ¾-inch seam allowance all around. Finally, from the batting, cut a main body piece that is ½ inch smaller than the pattern all around. To construct the body piece, place the two underside front paws and the tail-end section right sides together on the corresponding portion of the main body and join them with a ½-inch seam along the outside edges only. Turn this joined part of the body right side out, insert the batting piece, and stuff enough of the polyester stuffing into each paw to plump it out as shown in the photograph. Place the lining piece over the batting on the underside, turn under the raw edges, and sew it in place all around, stitching in from the side edges about ¼ inch so that the lining will not show when the finished bear is turned right side up and sewing through the double thickness of both the

59

lining and the batting. To assemble the head, first sew the back of each nose piece in position to the front head pieces, stitching on the wrong side of the work with a ¼-inch seam and clipping curves as necessary for the work to lie flat. Sew the center seam between the two sides of the front of the face, right sides together, stitching down the center of the head, around the nose, and under the chin. Then, right sides together, seam together the two back head pieces down the center and sew the back of the head to the front of the head, leaving the bottom edge open as indicated on the pattern. Seam two of the ear pieces together, right sides together, leaving the bottom seam open. Repeat for the other ear. Turn the ears to the right side, turn the bottom edges to the inside, and sew closed. Turn the head to the right side, stuff firmly, and sew the ears in position, curving them toward the back of the head, as shown in the photograph. Work the embroidery for the nose with the black yarn,

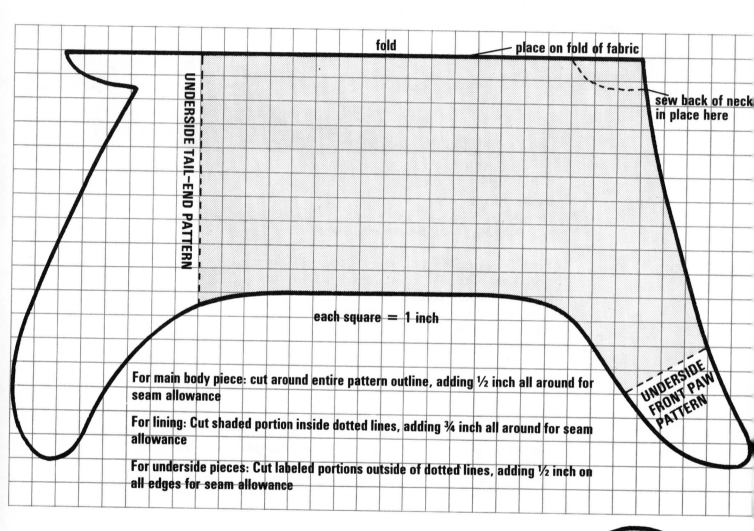

fold

place on fold of fabric

sew back of neck in place here

UNDERSIDE TAIL-END PATTERN

each square = 1 inch

For main body piece: cut around entire pattern outline, adding ½ inch all around for seam allowance

For lining: Cut shaded portion inside dotted lines, adding ¾ inch all around for seam allowance

For underside pieces: Cut labeled portions outside of dotted lines, adding ½ inch on all edges for seam allowance

UNDERSIDE FRONT PAW PATTERN

NOSE PATTERN
work in satin stitch
(actual size)

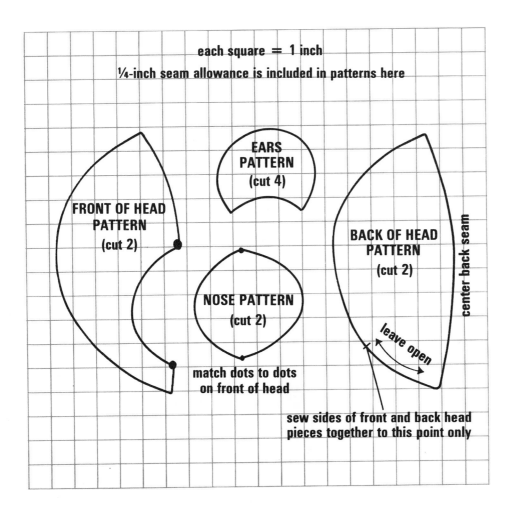

each square = 1 inch

¼-inch seam allowance is included in patterns here

EARS PATTERN
(cut 4)

FRONT OF HEAD PATTERN
(cut 2)

BACK OF HEAD PATTERN
(cut 2)

center back seam

NOSE PATTERN
(cut 2)

leave open

match dots to dots on front of head

sew sides of front and back head pieces together to this point only

using a satin stitch, as shown on the nose pattern. Sew the two black buttons in place for eyes and the red button in place for the mouth. Make a bow with the ribbon, tack the pompom in the center of it, and sew on bear's head as shown in photo. Now fold under ¼ inch of the remaining open portion at the bottom back of the head and sew this fold to the main body portion, as indicated on the pattern for the main body portion. Finally, stuff this neck portion firmly and close the remaining opening by sewing it in position to the main body piece.

Baseball Pete, An Oversized Doll Pillow

Big, tall, and outfitted in old-fashioned baseball stripes, ace pitcher Pete measures 11 inches × 24 inches and has just enough stuffing inside to make him a comfortable pillow for any Little Leaguer—a real friendly pillow, too.

Materials

brown wrapping paper
½ yard felt, 72 inches wide, in yellow
felt squares, each 10 inches x 10 inches, 2 squares in flesh tone, 2 squares in royal blue, 1
    square in white, and 1 square in brown
felt scraps in black and red
6 yards ribbon, ⅜ inch wide, in royal blue
small amount of 4-ply yarn in black
1 bag (1 pound) polyester stuffing
white glue

Pillow

On brown wrapping paper, enlarge the pattern including all the pattern markings, and cut it out. From the yellow felt, cut two pieces, following the main outline of

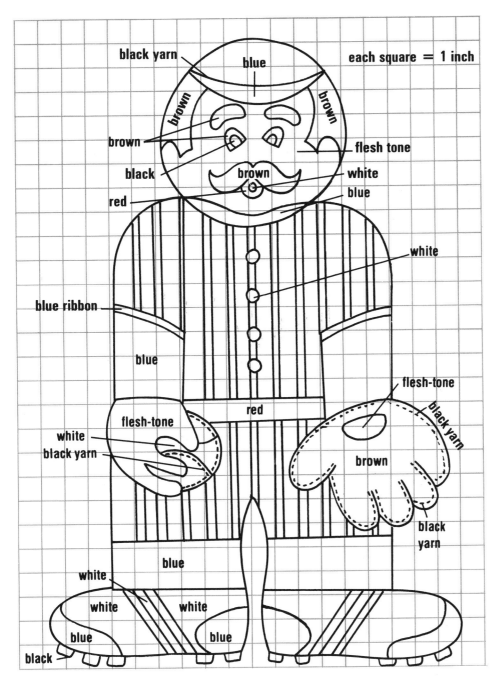

Vertical stripes on uniform and diagonal stripes on shoes-blue statin ribbon

the pattern only. Then, following the pattern for colors, trace each of the trimming shapes on the appropriate color of felt and cut them out, making sure to cut those that will overlap a bit larger than the pattern. Now sew the two main body pieces together around the outer edge, leaving an opening large enough through which to be able to insert the stuffing. Glue all the trimming pieces in place on one side of the pillow as well as the ribbon stripes and the black yarn that delineates the markings on the cap, glove, and ball, as shown on the pattern. Stuff the piece lightly so that it does not buckle and sew closed the remaining opening. To make the nose, cut a 1-inch-diameter disk from the flesh-colored felt, sew a gathering stitch around the outer edge, place a tiny amount of stuffing in the center of the piece, draw the thread up tightly, and fasten off. Glue the nose in place.

Cat and Mouse Games

Our two silly creatures, Patrick the Cat and Timmy the Mouse, are made in the simple single-crochet stitch. When finger-manipulated, they practically talk back to you—assuming they are not too busy fighting with each other.

Materials

1 ball (50 grams) medium-weight bouclé in white and 2 balls in burnt orange
aluminum crochet hook, size G
small amount of polyester stuffing
felt scraps in red, white, and black
small amount of black embroidery floss
pipe cleaner
white glue

Gauge in Single Crochet: 9 stitches = 2 inches

Timmy

Body (make two): Working in white single crochet throughout, work even on 18 sts for 6 inches. Then shape arms: Ch 9, work across 8 sts, work across the 18 body sts, then ch 9 and turn. Now work across 34 sts for 4 rows. On the next row, sl st across 8 sts, work to within the last 8 sts, and fasten off. *Head:* Ch 3, join with a sl st to form a ring, work 6 sc into the center of the ring, and on the next rnd, inc 1 st in each st around. Now inc 6 sts evenly spaced on every other rnd until there are 30 sc. Work even on these sts for 3 inches and fasten off. Fill the head with stuffing material, holding the stuffing in place by sewing a piece of felt over the open area. *Ears (make two):* With double strands of yarn, ch 3, join with a sl st to form a ring, then work 6 sc in the center of the ring, inc 6 sts on each rnd until there are 18 sts, and fasten off, leaving a small length of yarn with which to sew the ears to the head. *Tail:* With double strands of yarn, ch 25, then work 1 sl st in each ch across, and fasten off, leaving a small length of yarn with which to sew the tail to the body. *Finishing:* Sew the ears to the head, the body pieces together, the head to the body so that the nose points forward, as shown in the photograph, and the tail to the center back of the puppet. Work 1 row of sc along the foundation chain at the bottom of the puppet and fasten off. Trace the patterns for the facial features and tie as indicated on the pattern, cut corresponding pieces out of the appropriate colors of felt, and glue them in place; then embroider the whiskers with the black floss.

Patrick

Body and head (make two): With burnt orange yarn, work as for Timmy until there are 34 sts and then work even on these sts for 6 rows. On the next row, sl st across 11 sts, work to within the last 11 sts, ch, and turn. Work even now on 12 sts for 1 row and then shape head. Inc 1 st at beg and end of each of the next 3 rows; then work even on 18 sts for 6 rows. Finally, dec 1 st at beg of each of the next 5 rows and fasten off. *Ears (make two):* With double strands of yarn, ch 2 and turn. Work 2 sc in second ch from hook, ch 1, and turn. Then work 1 row even on 2 sts, ch 1, turn, inc 1 st at beg and end of every other row twice, work 1 row even on 6 sts, and fasten off, leaving a length for sewing. *Tail:* Work 2 rows of sc on 24 sts and fasten off. Then fold this piece lengthwise around a pipe cleaner and sew the edges together. Finish as for Timmy.

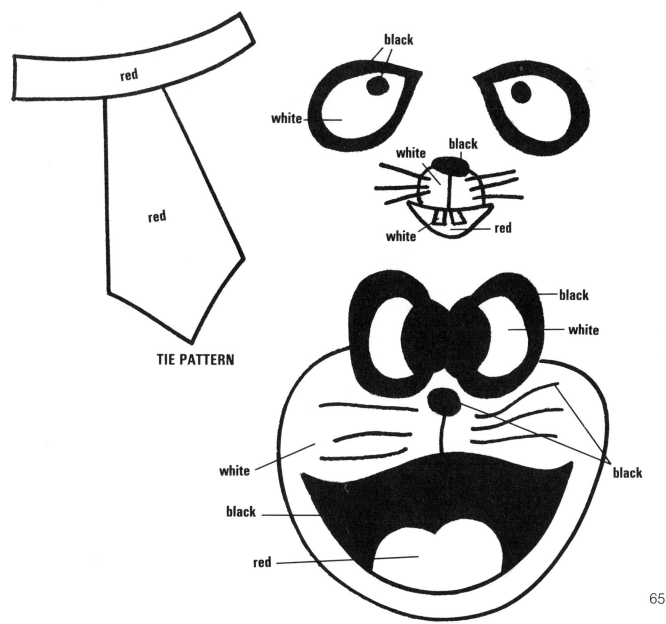

TIE PATTERN

Satin Stardust

A crescent moon, a cloud, and a star to dream by are shown here as they dangle from silvery threads to add a touch of the ethereal to a young lady's room.

Materials

brown wrapping paper
¼ yard heavy satin in each of light blue and white
1 skein embroidery floss in each of pink and blue
small amount polyester stuffing
few yards lurex thread in silver
few yards heavy-weight mohair yarn in a multicolor pastel
aluminum crochet hook, size G
dowel stick or other rod, 14 inches long, in white

Mobile

Enlarge all three patterns on the brown wrapping paper and cut them out. Use them to cut out the star from the blue satin and the cloud and moon from the white, following the pattern instructions and adding ½ inch all around each piece for a seam allowance. Stay-stitch ¼ inch in from the edges to prevent raveling. Then embroider the crescent moon and the cloud as shown on the patterns. Right sides together, sew together each set of two pieces now, leaving an opening for the stuffing. Turn the pieces right side out, stuff them firmly, and close the openings. Finally, using a single strand of the mohair and two of the lurex together, crochet two

66

8-inch-long chains, one each for the moon and the cloud, and one 12-inch-long chain for the star. Then sew one of each chain to the top of each piece and tie the other around the dowel. Make a 34-inch-long chain for hanging the mobile, again using the three strands of yarn together, and tie the ends around each end of the dowel.

MOON PATTERN (actual size)
(cut 2, reversing pattern for second piece)

blue stem stitch

blue stem stitch

blue satin stitch

pink stem stitch

pink stem stitch

blue stem stitch

STAR PATTERN (actual size)
(cut 2, reversing pattern for second piece)

CLOUD PATTERN (actual size)

(cut 2, reversing pattern for second piece)

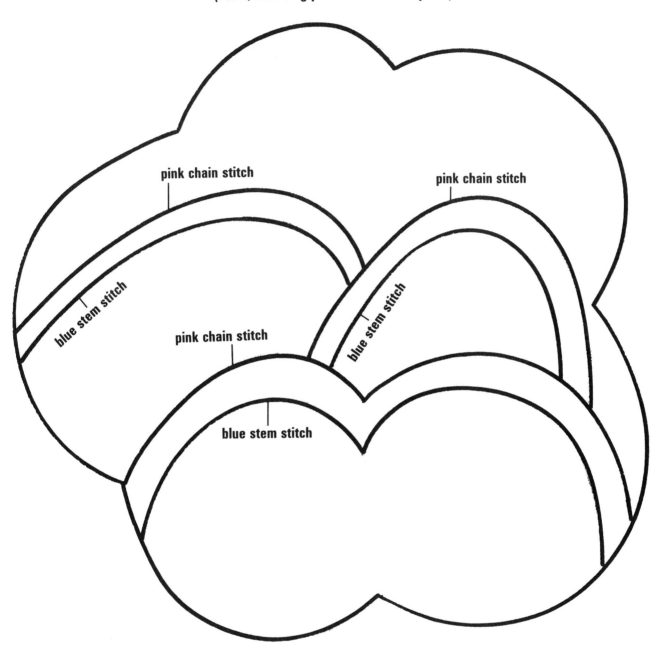

Star-sprinkled Helmet, Dickey, and Mitten Set

Star-studded for fun and closely knit for warmth, the pieces shown here are a rather unusual go-everywhere set of accessories. They're made with a soft blue yarn in the all-knit garter stitch, after which the red and white stars are appliquéd.

Materials

3 balls (4 ounces each) 4-ply knitting worsted in a medium blue
11 star appliqués in white and 5 appliqués in red, 1 inch across
1 button, ¾ inch in diameter, in blue
straight knitting needles, Nos. 4 and 6
aluminum crochet hook, size G

Gauge in Garter Stitch: 6 stitches and 12 rows = 1 inch

Helmet

With No. 6 needles, cast on 46 sts. Working in garter (knit every row), shape the piece as follows:* Dec 1 st at beg and inc 1 st at end of every other row 18 times; then inc 1 st at beg and dec 1 st at end of every other row 18 times. Now dec 1 st at beg and inc 1 st at end of every other row 13 times and then inc 1 st at beg and dec 1 st at end of every other row 13 times. End by repeating between *'s and binding off. *Finishing:* Sew the cast-on and bound-off edges together for the back seam. Seam the top increased and decreased edges as they fit together. Turn the center bottom point up for a 3½-inch cuff. Now work 2 rows of sc around the entire bottom edge of the piece, working the first row on the right side of both the cap and the center turned-up point and the second row from left to right instead of from right to left. Twist the excess of the seamed-together points at the top into a ball as shown and secure it in place by tying a strand of yarn tightly around the bottom of it. Finally, sew on five white and two red appliqué stars as shown or as desired. Then chain a buttonhole loop at the end of the portion that fits under the chin and sew a button to the other portion to correspond.

Dickey

With No. 6 needles, cast on 48 sts and work even in garter st for 10 inches. On the next row, work across 20 sts, join another ball of yarn, bind off the center 8 sts, and work across the remaining 20 sts. Working on both sides at once now, working each with a separate ball of yarn, dec 1 st at center edge every other row 5 times and then work even on 15 sts of each side for 2½ inches. Bind off. To make the turtle neck collar, cast on 20 sts with No. 4 needles, pick up and k 76 sts around the neck edge and then cast on 20 more sts. Work in k 1, p 1 ribbing for 4 inches and bind off in ribbing. *Finishing:* Sew back seam of collar. Work 2 rows of sc around the dickey, working this edging across the shoulders, along the two sides, and across the bottom. Finally, sew four white and three red appliqué stars on for trim as shown or as desired.

Mittens

Left mitten: With No. 4 needles, cast on 41 sts. Work k 1, p 1 ribbing for 2½ inches. Change to No. 6 needles and garter st and work even for 2½ inches more. *Divide for thumb:* Work across 17 sts, sl 7 sts on a holder, cast on 7 sts, and work across remaining 17 sts. Then work back and forth on all sts on needle for 2½ inches, ending with a wrong-side row and placing a marker on the center st of the last row. *Shape top:* On the next row, k 1, k 2 tog, k to within 2 sts of center marker, k 2 tog, k 1, k 2 tog, k to within last 3 sts, k 2 tog, k 1. Work the next row even. Rep these last 2 rows until 17 sts remain, then work 1 row even and bind off, leaving a long thread. Draw thread tightly through bound-off sts, and fasten off. *Thumb:* Work across 7 sts on holder, pick up the next thread between sts, pick up and k 1 st in each of the 7 cast-on sts, and pick up the next thread between sts. Work on the 16 sts on needle for 1¾ inches. *Shape top:* Dec 1 st at beg and end of every row 4 times; then bind off, leaving a long thread, draw thread tightly through bound-off sts, and sew thumb seam. *Finishing:* Sew side seam of mitten and, finally, sew one white star on the bottom, as shown. *Right mitten:* Work to correspond to left mitten, reversing the thumb shaping.

Soft Furnishings for a Doll's One-bedroom Apartment

Among our doll's new furnishings there is a reversible patchwork quilt and matching pillow, a dust ruffle and canopy, tie-back curtains, and a white high-pile area rug for the bedroom. For the living-dining area, there is a room-sized braided rug, a pair of decorative granny-square pillows, chair seat covers, and an embroidered tablecloth and matching curtains. All the pieces, finely detailed in a miniature 1-inch scale and worked in today's fashion colors, are really heirloom pieces—not only for a doll, but also for ourselves and our children.

Materials

1 piece rug canvas, 4 squares to 1 inch, 6 inches x 7 inches
masking tape
steel crochet hook, No. 10
2 ounces knitting worsted in white and 1 ounce each in camel and brown
¼ yard cotton fabric in each of white, orange, camel, and brown
small amount polyester stuffing
1 package binding tape, ½ inch wide, in brown
felt square, 10 inches x 10 inches, in brown
2 skeins embroidery floss in each of orange and brown
white glue

Bedroom

Rug (4½ inches × 6 inches): From the rug canvas, cut an oval that is 5½ inches × 7 inches. Then fold under ½ inch all around and secure the turnunder with masking tape to prevent it from raveling. Cut strands of white yarn to 3 inches long and, using the crochet hook, knot one strand in each square of the canvas. Trim ends evenly.

Quilt (6 inches × 7 inches): Cut sixteen 1-inch squares from each of the white, camel, orange, and brown fabrics; also cut a piece of brown fabric that is 6 inches × 7 inches for the backing. Then following the chart for the patchwork side of the quilt, arrange sixteen squares of each color in the pattern shown and sew them together on the wrong side of the work, stitching ⅛ inch in from the edges. Now, holding the patchwork front and the backing fabric together, right sides out and with a small amount of stuffing in between, sew them together with a running stitch, stitching through the three thicknesses and along all the edges of the joined squares. Finally, edge the entire piece with binding tape, sewing it on with an overcast stitch.

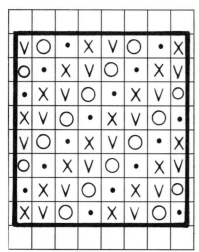

QUILT COLOR CHART

Color Key:

V = white
O = camel
• = brown
X = orange

Dust ruffle (4½ inches × 6¼ inches, without ruffle): From the white fabric, cut a piece that measures 5 inches × 6¾ inches. Turn under and press in a ¼-inch hem on all sides; sew down the hem on one short edge to make the top of the dust ruffle. For the ruffle, cut two pieces to 2¾ inches × 12 inches and one piece to 2¾ inches × 9 inches. Turn under and press a ¼-inch hem on each side of these pieces; sew in the hems on the two short edges and one long edge. Attach each ruffle separately to the body so that the corners will be open to fit around the legs of the bed. Gather each long ruffle to fit and then seam the raw edge to the corresponding long raw edge of the body, right sides together. Then, in the same way, gather and attach the shorter ruffle to the short edge of the body that has not been hemmed.

Canopy (5 inches × 7 inches without ruffle): Cut a piece of white fabric to measure 5½ inches × 7½ inches. Then work as for the dust ruffle except make two 2¾-inch × 12-inch pieces instead of one. Then sew the four ruffles along the four sides of the 5-inch × 7-inch piece, but seam the ruffles together at each point of joining instead of leaving them open.

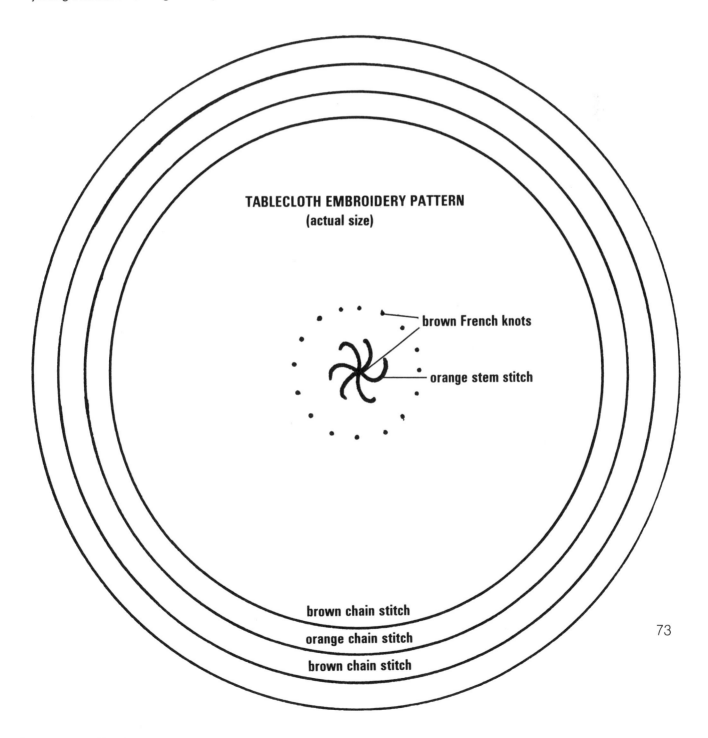

TABLECLOTH EMBROIDERY PATTERN
(actual size)

brown French knots

orange stem stitch

brown chain stitch

orange chain stitch

brown chain stitch

73

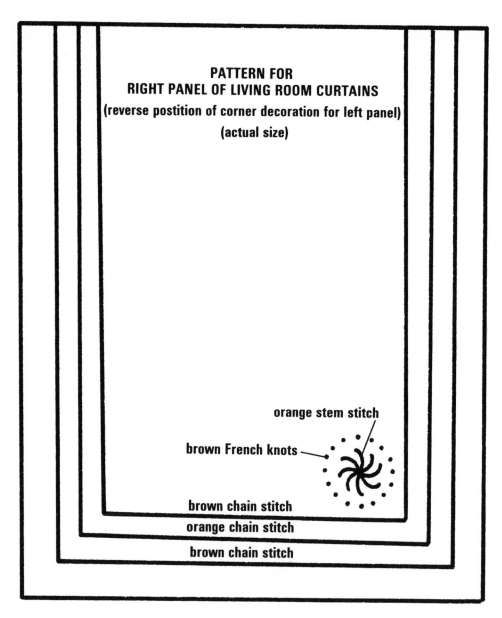

**PATTERN FOR
RIGHT PANEL OF LIVING ROOM CURTAINS**
(reverse postition of corner decoration for left panel)
(actual size)

orange stem stitch

brown French knots

brown chain stitch
orange chain stitch
brown chain stitch

Pillow: Cut two pieces of brown fabric, each measuring 1½ inches × 2½ inches, and one more for the ruffle that is ¾ inch × 12 inches. Sew the 1½-inch × 2½-inch pieces together, right sides out, stuffing the piece firmly as you sew. Then make a ⅛-inch-wide hem along each long side of the ruffle strip and sew the raw edge of the piece around the four sides of the pillow, gathering it to fit as you sew. Finally, sew the short ends of the ruffle together.

Tie-back curtains (make two pairs): For each pair, cut the white fabric into two pieces that measure 3 inches × 4½ inches for the panels, two 1½-inch × 16-inch pieces for the ruffles, and two 1¼ inch × 5-inch pieces for the tie-backs. Make a ⅜-inch hem all around each panel and ruffle piece, leaving one short edge on each panel open on the ends for casings. Turn under a ⅛-inch hem on the long sides of the tie-backs and press them in. Then fold each tie-back in half lengthwise and press. Finally, seam the edges along the outer long edge and lower short edge of each panel, gathering in the extra fullness as you stitch. Wrap a tie-back around each and tack the ends together.

Living-Dining Area

Braided rug: From brown felt, cut a disk that measures 8 inches in diameter. Then crochet chains in camel, brown, and white, each one long enough to glue into its position around the felt following the color pattern of 3 rows brown in the center, 2 rows white, 2 rows camel, 2 rows white, and two repeats of this using only 2 rows brown and ending with 2 more rows of brown around the outer edge of the felt. Finish the piece by trimming away any excess felt after the last 2 rows have been glued on.

Pair of granny-square pillows (make four pieces): With the brown, white, and camel knitting worsted split into single-ply lengths, work as follows: With brown, ch 6 and join with a sl st to form a ring. *Rnd 1:* Ch 3, (3 hdc in center of ring, ch 1) 3 times, 2 hdc in center of ring, join with a sl st to second ch of starting ch-3, and break off brown. *Rnd 2:* Attach white in first ch-1 sp of previous rnd, ch 3, work 3 hdc in first ch-1 sp (third ch of starting ch-3 of previous rnd), ch 3, then work 3 hdc, ch 1 in same sp, *(3 hdc, ch 1, 3 hdc) in next ch-1 sp, ch 1, rep from * twice, and end with 2 hdc in starting sp; join with a sl st to second ch of starting ch-3 and break off white. *Rnd 3:* Attach camel in first ch-1 sp of previous rnd, ch 3, and work 3 hdc in same sp, ch 1, *3 hdc in next ch-1 sp, ch 1, (3 hdc, ch 1, 3 hdc) in next ch-1 sp (corner), ch 1, rep from * twice, and end 3 hdc in next ch-1 sp, ch 1, 2 hdc in starting sp, join with a sl st to second ch of starting ch-3, and break off camel. *Rnd 4:* Attach brown in first ch-1 sp of previous rnd, ch 3, and work 3 hdc in first ch-1 sp, ch 1, *(3 hdc in next ch-1 sp, ch 1) twice, (3 hdc, ch 1, 3 hdc) in next corner ch-1 sp, ch 1, rep from * twice, and end (3 hdc in next ch-1 sp, ch 1) twice, 2 hdc in starting sp, join with a sl st to second ch of starting ch-3, and fasten off. To finish the pillows, sew them together with an overcast stitch, stuffing them firmly as you stitch.

Chair seat covers (make two): Trace the pattern on a piece of paper, cut it out, and use it to cut four pieces from the orange fabric. Turn under and press a ⅛-inch hem around each of the four pieces. Then sew each set of two together with an overcast stitch, right sides out, stuffing them lightly as you stitch. To finish them, crochet two 3-inch-long chains for each seat cover, using three strands of the orange embroidery floss. Tack the center point of each chain at a back corner of a seat cover to make ties.

Tablecloth: From the white fabric, cut a disk 7 inches in diameter, make a ⅛-inch hem all around, and then embroider it as shown on the pattern.

Curtains (make two): For the panels, cut two pieces from the white fabric, each 4½ inches × 5½ inches. Then make a ⅛-inch hem on the four sides of each piece and turn under and stitch a ½-inch-deep top casing on each. Embroider the pieces as shown on the pattern. Finish them by cutting a ⅞-inch × 7½-inch piece of white fabric for the valance and hemming it ⅛ inch on all four sides. Then tack it over the top edges of the curtains, leaving enough space between panels for it to cover the center of the rod on which it is to be hung.

CHAIR SEAT PATTERN
(actual size)

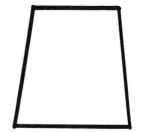

New Winter and Summer Ensembles for a Fashion Doll

Specially designed for Barbie®, or any of her fashionable 11-inch-tall friends, the wardrobe shown here will comfortably see her through both a winter and summer season. For cold weather, there is a warm, crocheted coat with a matching beret, a pair of boots, and a bright, contrasting scarf; and for summer and warm weather, there is a high-styled bikini, an embroidered sundress, and a pair of lace-up espadrilles.

Materials for the Winter Wardrobe

1 ball (50 grams) medium-weight bouclé yarn in camel and a small amount in orange
aluminum crochet hook, size G
2 snap fasteners
felt scrap in black
2 small wooden matches
white glue
black marking pen

Gauge in Single Crochet: 9 stitches = 2 inches

Coat

Working with the camel yarn in single crochet throughout, ch 25 and work on 24 sts for 4½ inches. Then working on what will be the right front only, work across 4 sts for 2 rows, dec 1 st at the front edge (neck) on each of the next 2 rows, work on 2 sts for 2 rows, and fasten off. Return now to row where shaping began, skip next 3 sts for the armhole, work on 10 sts for the back for 6 rows, and fasten off. Returning once more now to the row at the start of the shaping, skip the next 3 sts and work left front to correspond to the right front, reversing the shaping. *Sleeves:* Work on 8 sc for 2 inches, dec 1 st at beg and end of next row, work on 6 sts for 4 rows, work 3 sts tog twice on next row, then 1 row even on 2 sts, and fasten off. *Collar:* With right side of work facing, work 14 sc around the neck edge; then work on these sts for 6 rows and fasten off. *Finishing:* Work 1 rnd of sc around all outer edges of the coat. Sew shoulder seam. Seam the sleeves and sew them in place. For fringe, cut yarn into 3-inch-long strands. Knot two strands in each st around the bottom and sleeve edges, working 2 rows of the fringe along these edges and placing the lowest row 2 crocheted rows above the starting chain. Finally, sew on two snap fasteners for closing the coat, one at the neck edge and the other 2 inches below.

Beret

Working with the camel yarn and starting at the top, ch 3 and join with a sl st to form a ring. Work 6 sc in the center of the ring, then inc 6 sts on each rnd until there are 24 sts. Work 2 rnds even, dec 6 sts evenly spaced until there are 12 sts, work 1 rnd even on 12 sts, and fasten off.

Scarf

Working with the orange yarn, work even on 46 sts for 2 rows, work 1 rnd of sc around all four edges of the piece, and fasten off.

Boots

Trace the boot pattern on a piece of paper, cut it out, and use it to cut four pieces of black felt. Seam two matching pieces together on the right side of the material, leaving a ¾-inch opening at the top of the back; fold this portion over to the right side to make a cuff. Then color black one ¾-inch length of matchstick, insert it into the heel of the boot, and glue it in place. Repeat for the other boot.

Materials for the Summer Wardrobe

1 ball (250 yards) thin mercerized crochet thread in white and 1 ball in green
1 package baby rickrack in green
felt scrap in white
aluminum crochet hook, size B

Gauge in Single Crochet: 8 stitches = 1 inch

Sundress

Working with white in single crochet throughout and starting at the bottom, work even on 40 sts for 4 inches, then fasten off. Sew side seam, leaving the lower 1 inch open for a slit. *Straps:* With green, work 12 sc for 2 rows, work 3 sc in the last st of the last row, then work 1 more row of sc along the foundation chain, and fasten off. Repeat for the other strap. *Edging:* Work a green edging around the top and bottom edges of the sundress and along the slit as follows: Working 1 st in each st, work *2 sc, ch 3, 1 sl st in the first sc (picot made), rep from * around, and fasten off. *Finishing:* Sew straps to dress; then with green, embroider a row of lazy daisy sts with stem sts between diagonally across the front of the dress, as shown in the photograph.

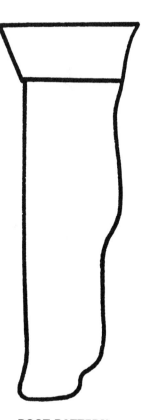

BOOT PATTERN
(actual size)
(cut 4)

Bikini

Bottom: Starting at the back with white and working in single crochet throughout, work on 12 sts for 2 rows; then dec 1 st at beg and end of every other row until 4 sts remain. Work even on 4 sts for 3 more rows and then inc 1 st at beg and end of every other row until there are 10 sts for the front portion. Finally, work 1 rnd of sc around the entire piece and fasten off. *Top (make two):* Work on 8 sts for 2 rows, then dec 1 st at beg and end of every other row until 2 sts remain, work off the 2 sts as 1 st, and fasten off. *Finishing:* Sew the two cups together at the bottom center only. Then make four 3-inch-long white chains and sew one at each corner of the bikini bottom for ties. Make two more 3-inch-long white chains and two that are 4 inches long. Sew one of the 3-inch chains to the top point of each cup and one of the 4-inch ones to each bottom side point. Tie the bottom chains together at the back, bring the 3-inch chains over the shoulders, cross them in the back, and tack each end in place ½ inch out from the center of the back. Finally, edge the top and bottom pieces with the rickrack, as shown in the photograph.

Espadrilles

Trace the sole pattern on a piece of paper, cut it out, and use it to cut four pieces of white felt. Then, with the white crochet thread, make two chains, each 20 inches long. Tack the center point of each of the chains between two sole pieces at the center back, sew each pair of soles together, and tie the chains around the legs as desired.

ESPADRILLE SOLE PATTERN
(actual size)

(cut 4)

A Personalized Wall Hanging

A joint venture for a little girl and her mom, this wall hanging is fashioned from "horserein" cords that are play for any child to make. Mommie can have her fun too in finishing the project by working out the initialed felt disks that hang from the cords and setting them up for hanging. The cords are made by using a spool knitter, available in the fabric or notions sections of variety and department stores.

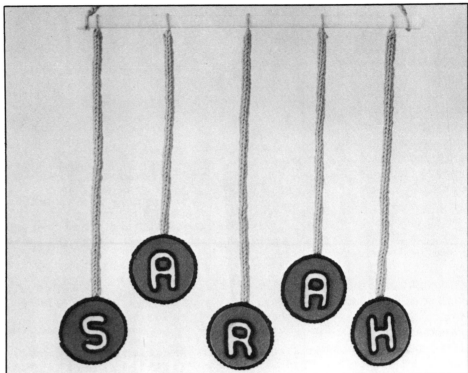

Materials

spool knitter

1 skein (4 ounces) 4-ply knitting worsted in aqua and 1 ounce in brown

¼ yard felt in aqua

felt scrap in white

sufficient medium-weight cardboard to make the same number of 2½-inch-diameter disks as the number of letters in the name to be spelled

aluminum crochet hook, size B

1 dowel stick or other rod, 14 inches long, in white

white glue

Wall Hanging

Following the instructions accompanying the spool knitter and using the aqua yarn, make as many horsereins of varying desired lengths as there are letters in the name to be spelled out, leaving an end of yarn long enough for tying each around the dowel rod. From the aqua felt, cut twice as many 2½-inch-diameter disks as the number of letters in the name. From the white felt, cut out freehand the desired letters, each small enough to fit comfortably within the aqua disks; then cut out the same number of 2½-inch-diameter disks from the cardboard as there are letters in the name. Glue each letter in the center of a felt disk and then glue that disk onto an untrimmed one, inserting a cardboard disk between the two. With the brown yarn, crochet one 55-stitch chain to fit around the outer edge of each initialed disk and glue it in place. Outline each letter by gluing a single strand of the brown yarn around it. Finally, sew each disk to the end of a horserein and add them, in proper order to spell the name, to the dowel by tying the opposite ends around the rod. Make a 22-inch-long crocheted chain with double strands of the aqua yarn and tie it to either end of the dowel for a hanging cord. Weight the untrimmed back of each disk by gluing on a drapery weight or a coin, if desired.

A Beribboned Tabard

Our tabard is made in a crisp, white crochet cotton beaded through with rows of pink satin and green rickrack. If made of a soft wool in a dark color, it could become a warm and attractive accessory to wear in winter, even over a sweater. The instructions for the one shown here are for a small size (26-inch to 28-inch chest); in parentheses, changes for a medium size (30-inch to 32-inch chest) are given.

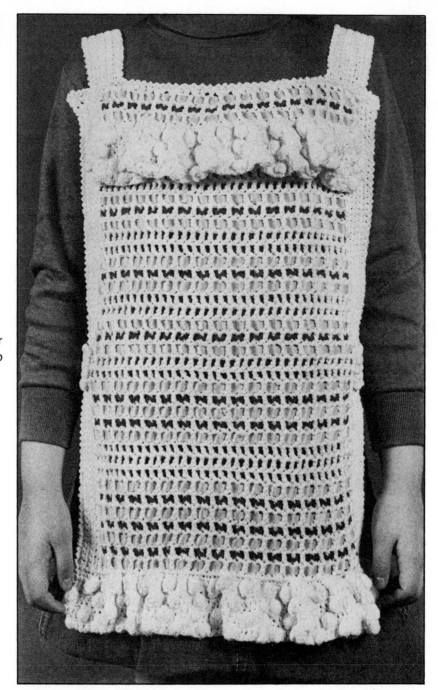

Materials

15 (17) balls (100 yards each) medium-weight mercerized crochet cotton in white
10 (12) yards satin ribbon, ¼ inch wide, in pink
4 (5) yards baby rickrack in green
aluminum crochet hook, size F
4 snap fasteners

Filet-Mesh Pattern Stitch: Row 1: Ch 5, 1 dc in sixth ch from hook, *ch 2, skip 2 ch, 1 dc in next ch, rep from * across row, ch 5, and turn. *Row 2:* Skip first dc, *1 dc in

Embroidered Crib Quilt with Bumpers and a Special Bib to Match,
p. 21; Andy, A Favorite Pet, p. 52.

Left to right: *A Beribboned Tabard, p. 80; New Winter and Summer Ensembles for a Fashion Doll, p. 76; Baseball Pete, An Oversized Doll Pillow, p. 62.*

Left to right: *A Norwegian Mesh Pullover for Him, p. 130; Pansy-sprigged Desk Accessories, p. 141; A Soft and Furry Dolman Slipover, p. 126; An Envelope Bag for On or Off the Shoulder, p. 112.*

Hazel, A Life-size Doll, p. 88.

the next dc, ch 2, skip 2 ch, rep from * across the row, and end with 1 dc in the third ch of the turning ch-5 of the previous row, ch 5, and turn. Repeat Row 2 for pattern.

Popcorn Pattern Stitch: Row 1: Ch 2, dc in fourth ch from hook and in each of the next 3 ch, *5 dc in the next ch, drop the lp from hook, insert hook in the first dc of the 5-dc group, pick up the lp and pull it through (one popcorn made), 1 dc in each of the next 5 ch, rep from * across the row, ch 1, and turn. *Row 2:* Work 1 sc in each dc and in each popcorn across the row and end with 1 sc in second ch of starting ch-2, ch 2, and turn. *Row 3:* Skip the first sc, 1 sc in the next sc, *popcorn in the next sc, 1 dc in each of the next 5 sc, rep from * across the row, and end with 1 dc in each of the last 2 sc, ch 1, and turn. *Row 4:* Rep Row 2. *Row 5:* Skip first sc, *1 dc in each of the next 4 sc, popcorn in the next sc, rep from * across the row, and end with 1 dc in each of the last 5 sc, ch 1, and turn. *Row 6:* Repeat Row 2. Repeat Rows 3 through 6 for pattern.

Gauge in Single Crochet: 6 stitches = 1 inch.

Tabard

Front and back panels (make two): Ch 70 (82) and work in the filet-mesh pattern until pieces measure 15 inches. End with 1 row of sc across the top, working 1 sc in each sc and in each sp across the row. Fasten off. *Side edgings:* On each side of each panel, work in sc for ¾ inch, working 1 sc in the base and in the spoke of each dc on the first row. *Top ruffles (make two):* Ch 66 (77) and then work 2 rows of sc, working the first row even on 66 (77) sts and increasing 1 sc in every sc except the last on the second row on the small size only (131, 154 sts). Now work in the popcorn stitch pattern for 12 rows and fasten off. *Bottom ruffles (make two):* Ch 77 (88) and then work 2 rows of sc, working the first row even on 77 (88) sts and increasing 1 sc in every sc on the second row (154, 176 sts). Work the 12 rows of the popcorn pattern stitch as for the top ruffles and fasten off. *Shoulder straps (make two):* Ch 64 and then work in sc on 63 sts for 1½ inches. Fasten off. *Side tabs (make two):* Ch 19 and then work in sc on 18 sts for 1½ inches. Fasten off. *Finishing:* On each piece, work 1 row of sc, working from left to right instead of from right to left, across the top and two side edges of the front and back panels and along the four sides of the shoulder straps and tabs. Bead the two panels, starting and ending each beading section with ribbon and alternating in between with rickrack, beginning at the bottom and working in the following pattern: 7 beading rows, skip 3 rows of spaces, 5 beading rows, sk 2 rows of spaces*, 3 beading rows, sk 2 rows of spaces, rep from * , and end with 3 beading rows. Tack the ends of the ribbons and rickrack strips to the wrong side of the work. Sew the top ruffles onto the panels, placing them 3 rows of spaces below the top edge. Then bead those rows with ribbon and rickrack in the same manner. Sew the bottom ruffles to the bottoms of the panel pieces. Then sew the shoulder straps in place, fitting them for comfort and stitching them under the top beaded rows. Next, place the tabs wherever they best fit the waist and sew them on over the side borders of the front panel so that they can connect the front to the back panel on each side. Finally, sew two snap fasteners to the loose end of each tab and their corresponding parts on the side borders of the back panels so that they can close the tabard.

A Fringy Fashion Jacket

The back and front of this girl's size 8 knitted jacket are heavily fringed in a stylish imitation of fur. A plain ribbed front band and collar with sleeves to match contrast with the fringe to further enhance the look. Instructions for making the jacket in sizes 10 and 12 are given in parentheses.

Materials

5 (6, 6) skeins (4 ounces each) knitting worsted in off-white
⅔ (1, 1) yard grosgrain ribbon, 1½ inches wide, in off-white
straight knitting needles, No. 10
aluminum crochet hook, size H
6 (7, 7) large snap fasteners

Pattern Stitch: Rows 1, 2, and 3: Knit. *Row 4:* *Yo, sl 1, k 1, pass sl st over the k st, rep from * across the row. Repeat these 4 rows for the pattern.

Gauge in Pattern Stitch: 4 stitches (unfringed) = 1 inch

Jacket

Back: Cast on 40 (44, 48) sts. Work the 4 pat rows 11 (12, 13) times. To shape armholes, bind off 4 (6, 6) sts at beg of each of the next 2 rows. Then continue to work even in pat on the remaining sts, repeating the 4 pat rows 5 (6, 7) times and ending with 1 row of knit sts. Bind off. *Left front:* Cast on 18 (20, 22) sts. Work the 4 pat rows 11 (12, 13) times. To shape armhole, bind off 4 (6, 6) sts at beg of next row, continue in pat across remaining sts, then rep Rows 1 through 4 on the remaining sts 5 (6, 7) times and *at the same time,* when the third (fourth, fifth) pat repeat has been completed, shape neck: Bind off 2 sts at front edge on next and every fourth row twice more and then work even until armhole measures same as back to shoulder. *Right front:* Work to correspond to left front, reversing all shaping. *Sleeves:* Cast on loosely 18 (22, 28) sts and work even in k 2, p 2 ribbing for 12½ (13½, 15) inches, increasing 1 st at beg and end of row every 1 inch 4 (5, 6) times. Then shape cap: Bind off 4 (6, 6) sts at beg of each of the next 2 rows and then dec 1 st at beg and end of every other row 4 (5, 7) times. Finally, bind off 2 (1, 3) sts at beg of each of the next 2 rows. When 6 (8, 8) sts remain, bind off. *Finishing: Front bands (make two):* Cast on 6 sts and work in k 2, p 2 ribbing for 11 (12, 13) inches; bind off. *Fringing:* Cut yarn into 5-inch-long strands and knot three in all vertical and horizontal bars across the back and fronts of the jacket except in the last horizontal rows on the shoulders and the first and last vertical bars at beg and end of the two front pieces. Sew side, sleeve, and shoulder seams. Sew in sleeves, easing in any extra stitches on the armholes, remembering that the ribbed sleeve stitches will stretch. Sew on front bands. *Collar:* With right side of work facing, pick up and k 60 (64, 68) sts around the neck and work in k 2, p 2 ribbing for 5 (5½, 6) inches; bind off loosely in ribbing. Line the front bands with the ribbon, and sew the snap fasteners equally spaced along the front bands to close. Trim fringe ends evenly. Work 1 row of sc, starting at the lower edge of the right front band and working up to the upper edge of the collar, across the long edge of the collar, down the left front edge, and around that lower front edge, working 3 sc in each corner st as you go.

Hazel, A Life-size Doll

Made to wear a size 6, 8, or 10 dress, Hazel could become a young girl's best friend. A child wearing any of these sizes can swap clothes with Hazel and if, with certain outfits, she feels that long brown braids would be more becoming to Hazel than her curly golden locks, she'll find it very easy to flip off one wig and change it for the other.

Materials

brown wrapping paper
2 yards cotton fabric, 45 inches wide, in flesh color
3 bags (1 pound each) polyester stuffing
2 yards elastic, approximately ¼ inch wide
2 skeins (4 ounces each) 4-ply knitting worsted in brown and 2 skeins
    in gold
2 ounces bulky yarn in red
cardboard
¼ yard felt in black
1 yard piping in black
½ yard braid, ½ inch wide, in black
2 snap fasteners
felt scraps in red, blue, green, and white
1 skein embroidery floss in black
white glue

Hazel

Body: On brown wrapping paper, enlarge the pattern pieces for the desired size of body, double the flesh-colored fabric, and, following the instructions on the patterns, cut out the pieces, adding ½ inch all around each piece for seam allowances. Now, right sides together, sew together the two torso pieces, two of the leg pieces, and then the other two leg pieces, leaving an opening in each for the turning and stuffing. Turn the pieces right side out and stuff them firmly. Close the openings and then sew the legs to the torso, making sure that the toes point forward.

Wigs: For each wig, make a fabric cap, following the front and back portions of the head marked off on the pattern and, again, adding ½ inch all around for a seam allowance. For each cap, cut a length of elastic to fit the head, seam the ends, fold the seam allowance over the elastic to form a casing, and hem it in place, For the brown wig, wind one full skein of the brown yarn around the length of a 20-inch x 8-inch strip of cardboard and, being sure to catch all the strands as you work, make a row of brown yarn chain stitches across the 8-inch width of the yarn to make a part in the hair. Then cut through the yarn loops on the opposite side of the cardboard, directly under the chain stitches worked. Remove the yarn from the cardboard and position the row of chain stitches vertically over the center back of the cap (place the cap on the doll's head for this fitting process). Now smooth the yarn over the rest of the cap to each side and braid each side, tacking hair to the cap wherever neces-

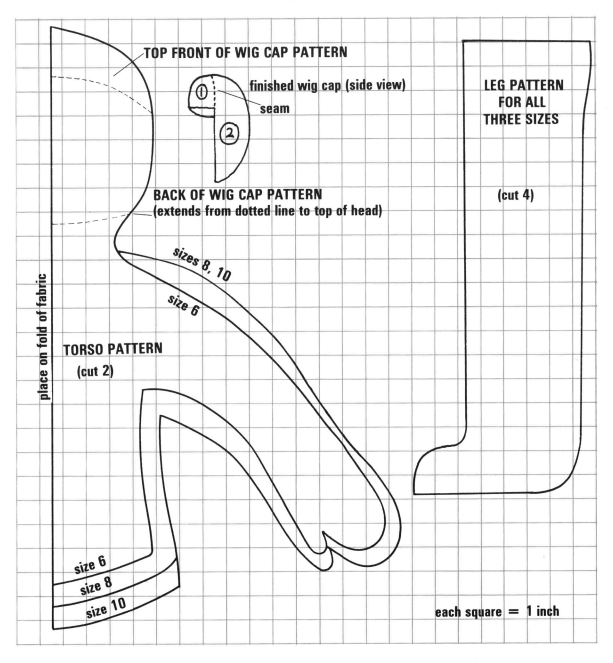

89

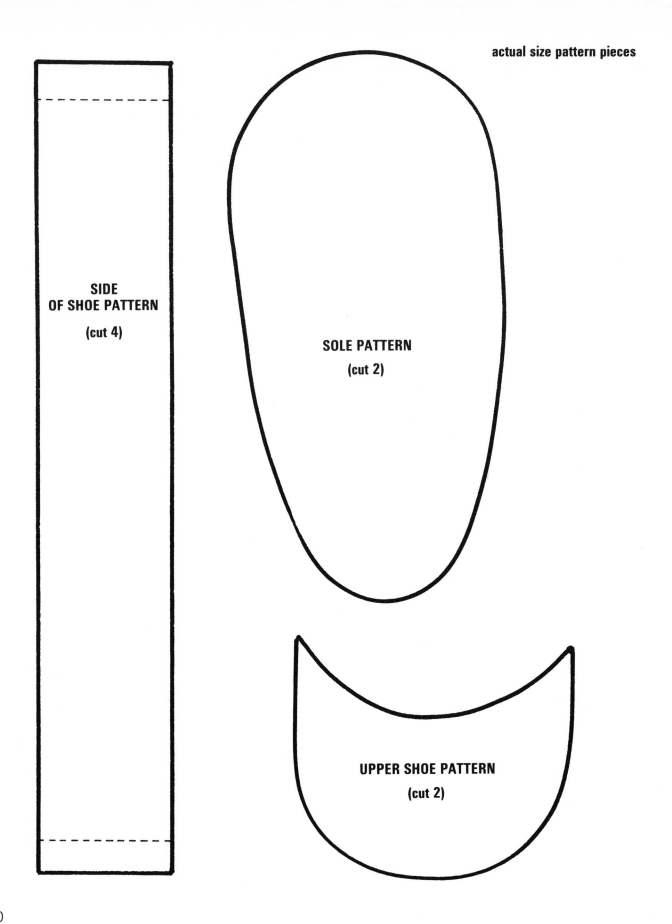

SIDE
OF SHOE PATTERN

(cut 4)

SOLE PATTERN

(cut 2)

UPPER SHOE PATTERN

(cut 2)

sary. To make the bangs, wind about half a skein of the brown yarn around a 10-inch width of cardboard over a 12-inch area. With more brown yarn, work a chain stitch straight across the 12-inch side of wound yarn, as for the braided section. Slip the yarn off the cardboard and, keeping all yarn loops toward the front of the face, center and sew down the row of chain stitches along the top seam of the cap. Now cut the loops, smooth down the bangs, and tack the hair to the cap wherever necessary. Finish by tying the end of each braid and each side of the bangs with a bow of the bulky red yarn. For the blond wig, make as many curls of the yellow yarn as are necessary to cover the entire top of the cap by winding a thick roll of the gold yarn around three of your fingers, making each roll approximately 1½ inches wide. Insert a short piece of yarn through the center of the roll and tie the ends to secure the roll. Then sew the curls to the cap, fluffing them a little with your fingers. Trim this wig with a red bulky-yarn bow sewn on each side.

Shoes: Trace the three pattern pieces for the shoes and cut two sole pieces from the cardboard. Then cut two sole pieces from the black felt slightly larger than the cardboard and glue these to the cardboard. Sew two of the side pieces to each sole, placing the seams at the center back and front of the shoe, sew the uppers in place, and finish the top edges by sewing piping around them. Finally, cut a length of the black braid to fit around each ankle and attach the center point of each braid to the center back of each heel of the shoes. Close each strap at the center front with a snap fastener.

Finishing: Add Hazel's features by tracing the pattern pieces for the eye, the mouth, and the nose and cutting them from the colors of felt indicated on the pattern pieces. Glue the pieces in place to the face. Then, embroider the upper and lower eyelashes around each eye with the black floss. Dress Hazel with a pair of socks and panties of desired choice and with a special dress, celebrating the surprise appearance of a new friend.

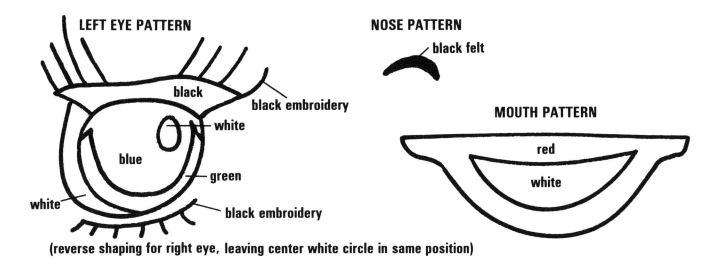

LEFT EYE PATTERN

black

black embroidery

white

blue

green

white

black embroidery

(reverse shaping for right eye, leaving center white circle in same position)

NOSE PATTERN

black felt

MOUTH PATTERN

red

white

actual size pattern pieces

Monogrammed Sleeping Bag for Overnight Fun

This reversible sleeping bag, made of a washable cotton polyester, is appliquéd on its bright, solid-color side with a monogram and a pair of little feet getting cold toes in the same gay, red calico that appears on the other side of the sleeping bag. Made for a child between five and eight or nine years old, the bag can be enlarged to adult size by making it 1½ feet longer and 1 foot wider. While ours is made for indoor overnights, the same bag, made in a nylon taffeta or heavy-duty canvas, would do well on overnight camping trips.

Materials

3 yards cotton polyester, 36 inches wide, in yellow
3¼ yards calico, 36 inches wide, in red
2 pieces polyester batting, each 81 inches x 96 inches
fabric glue
brown wrapping paper
2 ounces bulky yarn in black

92

Sleeping Bag

From the solid fabric, cut two pieces that are each 31 inches x 53 inches and two more pieces that same size from the calico. Then from each of the materials, cut eight 2-inch x 6½-inch pieces for the ties. From each piece of batting, cut five pieces that measure 21 inches x 52 inches. Join the long edges of the two yellow pieces with a ½-inch seam; repeat with the two calico pieces. To make the ties, place pairs of same-color pieces right sides together and seam them along three sides, leaving one short end open; then turn the pieces right sides out. Now place the large, joined solid and print pieces right sides together with the solid piece on top, place the ties between the layers, open edges out, as shown on the diagram, and make a ½-

top

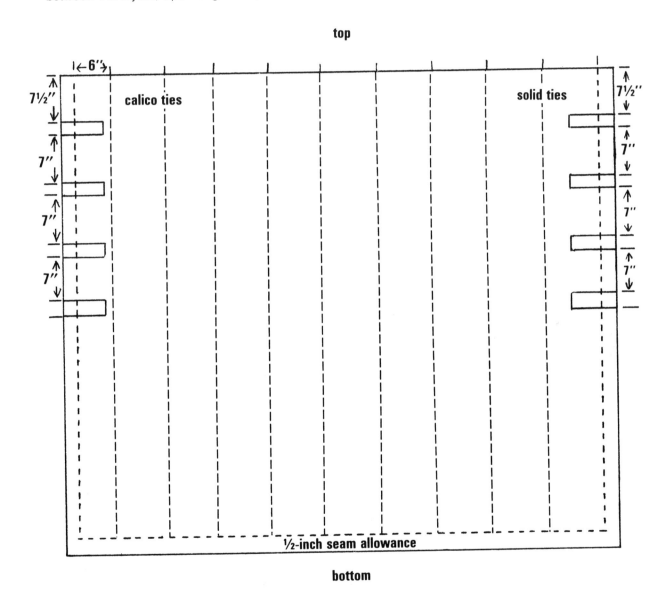

bottom

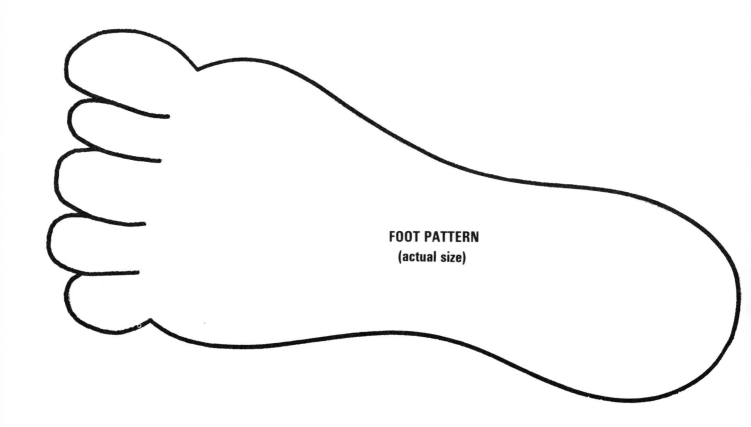

FOOT PATTERN
(actual size)

inch-wide seam around the three sides of the piece indicated on the diagram—this also secures the tabs in place. Turn the piece right side out and mark off on it ten 6-inch-wide sections, as shown on the diagram. Then, working one piece at a time, fold the 21-inch x 52-inch batting strips in three, each now measuring 7 inches x 52 inches. Fit and pin the first strip within the first 6-inch-wide marked-off section and then topstitch that section along the length of the batting, sewing through the two layers of fabric only to within 1 inch of the top, open edge. Repeat this step with the remaining nine sections. Next, on both large pieces of fabric, fold to the inside ½ inch of fabric along the top, open edge of the sleeping bag and topstitch the two pieces together. Then fold the entire piece in half so that it is 30 inches wide and the solid-color side is up. Topstitch across the bottom edge; join the open side edges by topstitching the lower 14 inches of them together. *Finishing:* Cut four 1-inch x 52-inch strips of the calico material, fold ¼ inch of each long edge of each strip to the underside, press the folds in place, and glue one strip over each topstitched line on the top of the bag, as shown in the photograph. Draw and cut three 3½-inch x 5½-inch letters of your choice from the calico and glue them in place, as shown in the photograph. Then trace the foot pattern on brown wrapping paper, cut it out, and use it to cut a left foot from the print fabric; reverse it to cut a right foot. Glue both in place, as shown in the photograph. Finally, outline the letters and the feet, including the toes, with a single strand of the bulky yarn, gluing it in place first and then securing it by whipstitching over the yarn with sewing thread.

2

For Big People

Strictly for After Dark, A Sequined Cap and Scarf Duet

Silver sequins here add sparkle to a long, jet black scarf and shiny matching cap that look to the elegant Deco period for their inspiration. Very easy to make in the single-crochet stitch, the set, worked up in any desired color, can provide the coup de grace to any dramatic evening wear.

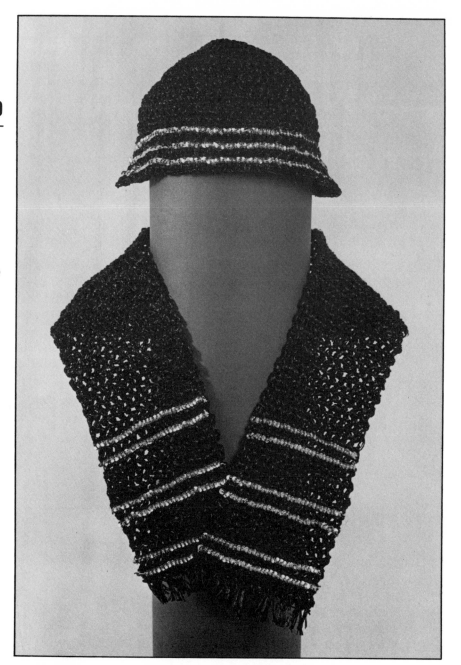

Materials

4 balls (50 grams each) lightweight straw or other novelty yarn in black
4 balls (100 yards each) medium-weight mercerized crochet cotton in black
3 yards small strung sequins in silver
aluminum crochet hook, size I

Gauge in Single Crochet: 3 stitches = 1 inch

96

Cap

Using one strand of the novelty yarn and one of the cotton together, ch 7, turn, and then work 1 row of sc on 6 sts. Working in sc throughout, on the next row, inc 1 st in each st across (12 sc). *Next row:* *Sc in the first st, 2 sc in the next, rep from * across the row (18 sc). *Next row:* *Sc in each of the next 2 sts, 2 sc in the next, rep from * across (24 sc). Continue now to inc 6 sts evenly spaced on each row until there are 60 sts and piece measures approximately 3 inches, measuring from the top straight down. Then work even for 3 more inches. *Shape bottom:* Work in sc across 9 sts, *2 hdc in each of the next 2 sts, 2 dc in each of the next 7 sts, 2 hdc in each of the next 2 sts,* 1 sc in each of the next 20 sts, rep from between *'s, work 1 sc in each of the last 9 sts, and fasten off. *Next row:* Work 1 sc in each sc and 1 sc in every other dc and hdc across the row. *Finishing:* Sew back seam. Then sew three rounds of the strung sequins around the bottom of the cap, the first round one row above the bottom row and the remaining two each two rows apart.

Scarf

Using one strand of each yarn together, ch 15 and then work even in sc until piece measures 54 inches; fasten off. *Finishing:* Cut an equal number of strands of the novelty yarn and the crochet cotton, each 2½ inches long. Using one strand of each together, knot them in every stitch along both short ends of the scarf. Then sew three double rows of sequins across each end, positioning the first half of the first double row two rows above the fringe and the second half two rows above that one. Skip four rows and add the next two rows of sequins; skip four more rows and add the last two.

Personalized, An Oversized Beret Knitted of Mohair

Big, black, and initialed for your very own, the beret here is simply made. The monogram is added to the beret afterwards by going over iron-on appliqué initials with embroidery floss and a satin stitch.

Materials

3 balls (50 grams each) medium-weight mohair yarn in black
3 skeins embroidery floss in medium blue
3 iron-on initials, each approximately 1¼ inches wide ×
    1½ inches high
straight knitting needles, Nos. 4, 6, 8, and 10

Gauge in Stockinette Stitch: 3 stitches = 2 inches on No. 10 needles

Beret

With No. 8 needles, cast on 42 sts and work in k 1, p 1 ribbing for 1½ inches. Then change to No. 10 needles and k the next row, increasing 12 sts evenly spaced on this row. P the next row on 54 sts. Continue to k 1 row and p 1 row (stockinette st) on 54 sts until piece measures 5½ inches in all, ending with a p row. Change to No. 8 needles, p the next row, and k the next (reverse stockinette st). Continuing in this pat st throughout, work even for 4 rows, change to No. 6 needles, dec 1 st at beg and end of the next row, and work even on 52 sts for 1 more row. Now change to No. 4 needles, dec 4 sts evenly spaced on the next row, work 1 more row even on 48 sts, and then, continuing with No. 4 needles, dec 6 sts evenly spaced on every other row until 6 sts remain; break off yarn, leaving a long thread. *Finishing:* Thread the strand of remaining yarn into a needle, draw through the remaining 6 sts on the needle, and sew the back seam. Now block beret into shape, iron your initials in place, and embroider over them with the embroidery floss using a satin stitch.

A Long, Skinny Boa

Measuring a long 80 inches and a very narrow five inches, this elegant accessory is made of a medium-weight bouclé yarn crocheted into a filet-mesh base and fringed on both the wrong and right sides with uneven lengths of the same yarn, interspersed with metallic strands to add a shimmer to the very interesting shaggy effect.

Materials

8 balls (40 grams each) medium-weight bouclé in white
1 ball (1 ounce) medium-weight metallic twist yarn in silver
aluminum crochet hook, size H

Pattern Stitch: Row 1: Ch 4, dc in fifth ch from hook, *ch 1, skip 1 ch, dc in the next ch, rep from * across the row, and end with 1 dc in the last ch, ch 3, and turn. *Row 2:* *Skip 1 dc, dc in the next dc, ch 1, rep from * across the row, and end with 1 dc in the third ch of the starting ch-4, ch 3, and turn. *Row 3:* *Skip 1 dc, dc in the next dc, ch 1, rep from * across the row, and end with 1 dc in the second ch of the turning ch-3, ch 3, and turn. Repeat Row 3 throughout for the pattern.

Gauge in Pattern Stitch (before fringing): 4 double crochet and 3 spaces = 2 inches; 3 rows = 2 inches

Boa

With the bouclé, ch 11. Work even in pat until piece measures 74 inches. Fasten off. *Fringing:* Cut the bouclé into strands, cutting equal amounts of 9-inch, 8-inch, and 7-inch lengths; then cut strands of the silver yarn, all 9 inches long. Mixing the different lengths of the bouclé yarn at random and starting at the bottom and working on the right side of the finished piece, *knot five strands in each of the first 3 spaces, four strands of the bouclé and four of silver in the next, and repeat from * for the entire length of the piece, keeping the fringing pattern consecutive throughout and skipping every other row of spaces as you go. When this portion of the work has been completed, turn the piece to the wrong side and fringe it in the same manner along those rows not fringed on the right side. *Note:* Do not trim the fringe ends when done, for the shaggy look is part of the boa effect and the strands hanging from the first fringed row add to the length of the boa.

Plaid Scarf Knitted in Tartan Colors

Long and narrow, knitted vertically, and worked in Scotch plaid colors of red, dark navy, and gold, our scarf is easy to make for anyone who knows the basic knit and purl stitches.

Materials

**1 skein (4 ounces) knitting worsted in scarlet (A), 1 skein
 in navy (B), and 2 ounces in gold (C)**
straight knitting needles, No. 8
aluminum crochet hook, size E

Gauge in Stockinette Stitch: 7 stitches = 2 inches

Scarf

With A, cast on 188 sts. Working in stockinette st throughout (k 1 row, p 1 row), work in color pat as follows: *6 rows A, 4 rows B, 2 rows C, 4 rows B, rep from *once, and end with 6 rows A; bind off. To complete the plaid pattern, embroider with C and a chain st double horizontal stripes across the width of the piece, allowing 2 rows between each stripe in the pair, 2½ inches between each pair, and approximately 3½ inches before the first and after the last stripe at the ends of the scarf. *Finishing:* Cut a number of strands of colors A, B, and C, each 11 inches long. Working color over color and using two strands for each, knot four strands in each color A stripe, three in each B, and one in each C across the short ends of the scarf. Finally, work 1 row of color A single crochet along each long edge.

Silky, Tasseled Neckwear

Tasseled at both ends and measuring a narrow 4½ inches in width and a long 68 inches, this gleaming, vertically striped scarf is a very important accessory for blazers and jackets, although it's been designed more for "show" than for a big "blow."

Materials

3 balls (50 grams each) lightweight straw or other novelty yarn in bronze (MC) and 2 balls each in sapphire (A) and orange (B)
aluminum crochet hook, size H

Gauge in Single Crochet: 4 stitches = 1 inch

Scarf

Starting with MC and working in sc throughout, ch 273 sts. Then work even in sc on 272 sts for 6 rows, break off MC, attach color A, and work 2 rows with A. Continuing to break off yarn before starting each new stripe, work 2 rows B, 2 rows A, 4 rows MC, 2 rows A, 2 rows B, 2 rows A, 6 rows MC, 1 row of sl st with MC, and fasten off. *Finishing:* Turn the scarf to the wrong side. Starting 4 inches back from each short end, fold the ends in so that they taper from the 4-inch width to 1 inch, and stitch tapered ends in place. Make two tassels by cutting an equal number of A and B strands of yarn, each 10 inches long, folding them in half, and tying them together through the center point. Then tie them again 1 inch below the center point and once more 2 more inches below that. Finally, sew one tassel to each of the squared-off, 1-inch-wide ends of the scarf.

Granny-Square Cap and Scarf Set

Bright, colorful, crocheted "grannies" are joined together to shape the cap and scarf set shown here, made just a little different with the striped, quadruple roll-over cuff on the cap and the striped trim and random placement of the squares on the scarf.

Materials

3 skeins (4 ounces each) 4-ply knitting worsted in navy (MC),
1 skein in white (A), and 2 skeins in coral (B)
aluminum crochet hook, size F

Granny Squares: With MC, ch 6 and join with a sl st to form a ring. *Rnd 1:* With MC, ch 6 (counts as 1 dc and ch 3), *1 dc in center of ring, ch 3, rep from * 6 times, join with a sl st to third ch of starting ch-6; fasten off. *Rnd 2:* Attach A in any ch-3 sp, ch 2, 3 dc in same ch-3 sp, ch 2, *4 dc in next ch-3 sp, ch 2, rep from * around, and join with a sl st to second ch of starting ch-2; fasten off. *Rnd 3:* Attach B in any ch-2 sp, ch 2, 5 hdc in same ch-2 sp, ch 1, *6 hdc in next ch-2 sp, ch 3, 6 hdc in next ch-2 sp, ch 1, rep from * twice, and end with 6 hdc in next ch-2 sp, ch 3, join with a sl st to second ch of starting ch-2; fasten off. *Rnd 4:* Attach MC in any ch-3 sp, ch 5, skip 3 hdc, *1 sc in sp before next hdc, ch 3, 1 sc in next ch-1 sp, ch 3, skip 3 hdc, 1 sc in sp before next hdc, ch 3, (2 dc, ch 3, 2 dc) in next ch-3 sp, ch 3, skip 3 hdc, rep from * twice, and end 1 sc in sp before next hdc, ch 3, 1 sc in next ch-1 sp, ch 3, skip 3 hdc, 1 sc in sp before next hdc, ch 3, (2 dc, ch 3, 1 dc) in next ch-3 sp, join with a sl st to second ch of starting ch-5, and fasten off.

Gauge: 1 granny square = 4 inches; 4 single crochet = 1 inch

Cap

Make five granny squares and then sew them together into a ring. To shape top, attach MC into any seam stitch and work 60 sc evenly spaced around one edge of the ring. Then continuing in rnds, work as follows: *Rnd 1:* *Sc across 5 sts, skip 1 st, rep from * around. *Rnd 2:* Work even. *Rnd 3:* *Sc across 4 sts, skip 1 st, rep from * around. Continue in this manner, decreasing 10 sts evenly spaced on every other rnd and working all alternate rnds even, until 20 sts remain. *Next rnd:* Work 2 sts tog around. *Next rnd:* Work even. Rep last 2 rnds once and then break off yarn, leaving a long thread. Draw the thread through remaining sts, pull up tightly, and fasten off. *Shape cuff:* With MC, work 60 sc evenly spaced around the bottom of the cap. Working even throughout, work back and forth in sc for 2 inches, then alternate 1 row B and 1 row MC for 5 inches more, and fasten off. *Finishing:* Sew back seam; fold cuff in half and then in half again.

Scarf

Make fifteen granny squares and then make ten MC inserts as follows: Ch 7, work in sc on 6 sts for 4 inches, then work back and forth on 3 sts only for another 4 inches, and fasten off. Arrange the granny squares and inserts as shown on chart and join them together with an overcast stitch. *Finishing:* With wrong side of work facing, attach MC in one corner of the scarf. Then work 1 row of sc along one long edge (working a sufficient number of sts so that the work lies flat), 1 row of color B, 1 more row of MC, and then 1 row of sc in MC, working from left to right instead of from right to left; fasten off. Complete the other long edge of the scarf to correspond. Finally, work 1 row of MC sc along each short end of the scarf and knot two 16-inch-long strands of yarn for fringe in each sc along each of these short ends.

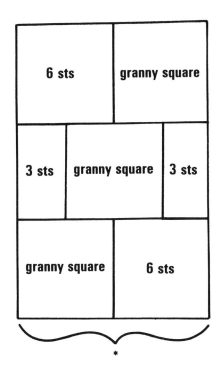

SCARF PATTERN
repeat from * four times more

A Cap, Scarf, and Leg-warmer Set Trimmed with Bolts of Lightning

It is said that lightning strikes only once, but in the cap, scarf, and leg-warmer set shown here, it strikes three times in the form of white, navy, and orange fringe striped across a coppery background. Crocheted in a knitting worsted yarn, these colorful pieces can be great fun worn together as a set or separately, depending on how dramatic you feel.

Materials

3 skeins (4 ounces each) 4-ply knitting worsted in copper brown
  and 1 skein in each of white, navy, and orange
aluminum crochet hook, size G

Gauge in Single Crochet: 4 Stitches = 1 inch

Cap

Starting at the top and working in copper brown sc throughout, ch 6. Then, working back and forth, inc 6 sts evenly spaced on every row until there are 84 sts. On the next row, dec 4 sts evenly spaced. Then work even on 80 sts for 18 rows, work 1 row through the back lps only of the sts to make a turnover row, work 13 more rows in the usual way, and fasten off. Turn up the cuff. To finish the cap, cut 4-inch-long strands of each of the other colors of yarn and knot two in every stitch, following the color and placement chart and making sure that the fringe is placed on the outside of the cuff. Then sew the back seam of the cap.

Scarf

Working in copper brown sc throughout, work even on 25 sts for 60 inches and fasten off. To finish, knot two strands of 4-inch-long fringe at both ends of the scarf as on the cap but following the color and placement chart for the scarf.

Leg-warmers

The instructions here are written for a short length; changes for medium length and long are also given, in parentheses, for those who desire more warmth. Working in copper brown sc throughout, work even on 40 (42, 44) sts for 10 (11, 12) inches. Then inc 1 st at beg and end of every other row four times—48 (50, 52) sts. For the medium length, work 4 more rows even; for long, work 8 more rows even. For all sizes now, work 1 row even through the back lps only of the sts to make a turnover row, *at the same time* decreasing 8 (10, 12) sts evenly spaced across the row. Then work 13 more rows for the cuff and fasten off. To finish, turn the cuff over and fringe it as indicated on the chart. Then sew the back seam, including the cuff if desired. Repeat for the other leg-warmer. Add a strip of elastic across the bottom of each leg-warmer (from side to side) if desired to keep them in place.

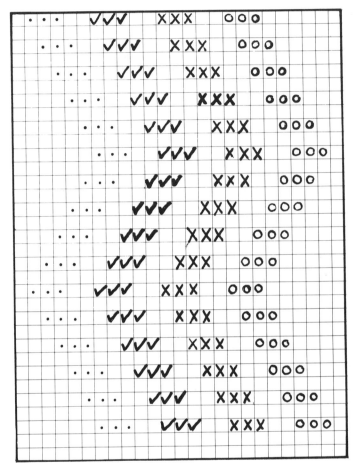

SCARF

Color Key:

0 = white

• = orange

✓ = copper brown

x = navy blue

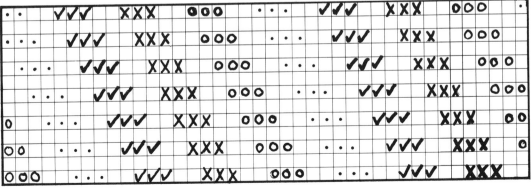

LEG-WARMERS

FOR HAT, REPEAT TWICE

For Him, An Icelandic Cap and Scarf

Very warm because it's knitted with long-haired, Icelandic yarns, this cap and scarf set could make a great gift for any man. Designed basically in a soft beige, the scarf and cap are accentuated with a pattern worked in the natural, undyed colors of charcoal brown, light brown, and off-white.

Materials

4 balls (50 grams each) Icelandic Homespun in soft beige (MC) and 1 ball in each of charcoal brown (A), light brown (B), and off-white (C) straight knitting needles, Nos. 8 and 10

Pattern Stitch: Rows 1 and 2: *K 2, p 2, rep from * across the row, and end with k 1. *Rows 3 and 4:* *P 2, k 2, rep from * across the row, and end with p 1. Repeat Rows 1 through 4 for pattern.

Gauge in Pattern Stitch: 5 stitches = 1 inch

Cap

With No. 8 needles and MC, cast on 101 sts. Work in k 1, p 1 ribbing for 5 inches. Change to No. 10 needles and pat st, and work for 4 rows with MC, 4 rows with color A, 4 rows with B, 4 rows with C, 4 rows with B, and 4 rows with A. Then shape top: Working in MC stockinette st (k 1 row, p 1 row) to completion, dec 5 sts evenly spaced on the next row. Work the next 3 rows even. Then *k 6, k 2 tog, and rep from * across the row. Work the next 3 rows even. On the next row, *k 5, k 2 tog, rep from * across the row. Continue now in this manner to dec 12 sts evenly spaced on every fourth row until 12 sts remain. Work 1 row even and then on the next row, k 2 tog across. Break off yarn, leaving a long thread. *Finishing:* Draw thread at top through remaining sts and sew back seam. To make the top button, with No. 10 needles and MC, cast on 7 sts. Working in stockinette st, work 2 rows even. Then inc 1 st at beg and end of next row, work 1 row even, rep last 2 rows once more, work 1 row even, and then dec 1 st at beg and end of every other row until there are 7 sts; bind off. Draw a strand of yarn loosely through the four sides of this piece, stuff the center of it lightly with enough scrap strands of yarn to make it firm, pull the gathering strand tight, and, with the same strand, sew the button to the top of the cap.

Scarf

With No. 10 needles and MC, cast on 40 sts. Continuing in pat st throughout, work in MC for 5¾ inches. Then work *4 rows with color A, 4 rows with B, 4 rows with C, 4 rows with B, and 4 rows with A*, 44 inches with MC, rep from between *'s, and end with 5¾ inches MC. Fasten off.

Pattern-knit
Guitar Strap

Functional—yet still a great gift for anyone who likes to play the guitar—the sturdy knitted strap shown here measures 46 inches, although its length can be adjusted for personal comfort.

Materials

**1 skein (4 ounces) knitting worsted in taupe and 2 ounces each
   in gold and burnt orange**
1 strip lining fabric, 5½ inches x 47 inches, in taupe
1 strip heavy rug canvas, 2½ inches x 46 inches
straight knitting needles, No. 9
heavy-duty thread in taupe
1 shoelace in brown

Gauge in Stockinette Stitch: 4 stitches = 1 inch

Strap

With taupe, cast on 21 sts and, repeating the color pat given in the chart, work even in stockinette stitch until piece measures 46 inches, or the desired length for a comfortable playing position, working the last 2 rows in taupe and making a button hole 1 inch before reaching the end of the strip by binding off the center stitch on a knit row and casting on 1 stitch over the bound-off one on the following purl row. Bind off. *Finishing:* Wrap the strip of lining material around the canvas and seam it at the center back, first turning under a ¼-inch seam allowance on each edge. Turn in the short edges of the strip and hem them in place. Wrap the knitted strip around the lined canvas and seam it at the center back, cutting a buttonhole through the covered canvas strip to correspond to the knitted buttonhole and overcasting it together with the knitted one. Seam the short end closest to the buttonhole. Finally, lay the center portion of the shoelace along the remaining open short edge and sew it in place. Then sew this edge of the knitted strip closed, leaving an end of the lace extending at each side. Tie these ends to the neck of the guitar, and insert the knob at the bottom of the instrument into the buttonhole at the other end of the strap.

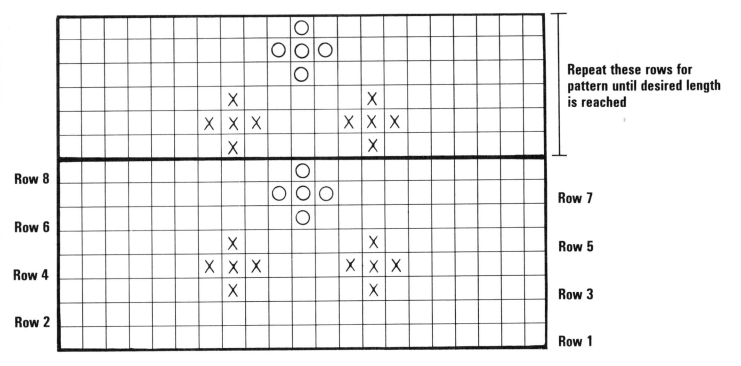

Repeat these rows for pattern until desired length is reached

Row 8   Row 7

Row 6   Row 5

Row 4   Row 3

Row 2   Row 1

Color Key:

☐ = **taupe**
X = **burnt orange**
0 = **gold**

A Versatile Obi Sash

Designed for dressing up, our obi is made of a black and silver metallic cloth and finished with crocheted bands of silver yarn. For less formal wear, it could be made of a heavier material, or lightweight leather, with ties made of an appropriate yarn. Not only is the choice of fabric up to you, but also the way you wear it—you can criss-cross the bands in the front and tie them in the back, or you can simply bring them around to the front and tie them in a bow, allowing the long ends to hang down gracefully.

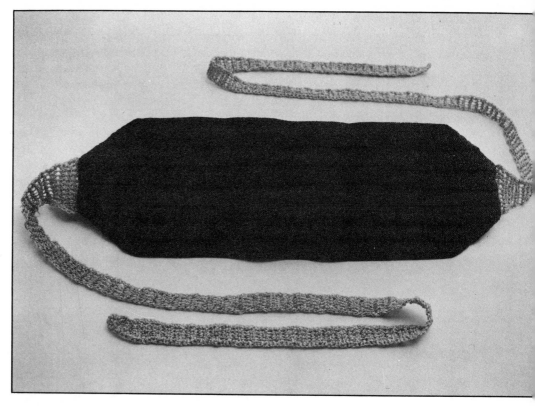

Materials

⅔ yard metallic fabric, 36 inches wide, in black and silver
¼ yard stiff buckram or interfacing, 36 inches wide
1 ball (50 grams) metallic yarn in silver
aluminum crochet hooks, sizes C and H

Gauge in Single Crochet: 5 stitches = 1 inch on size H hook

Obi

Cut a piece of fabric 21 inches x 22 inches and a piece of buckram according to the cutting diagram. With right sides together, join the two 22-inch edges of the fabric with a ½-inch seam. Turn the piece right side out and slip the finished cylinder

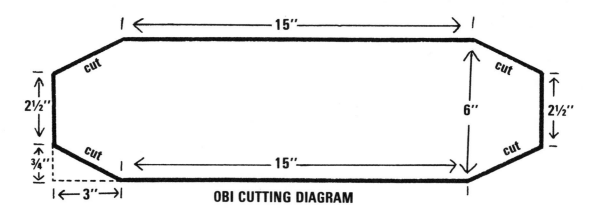

OBI CUTTING DIAGRAM

of fabric over the buckram, centering the seam along the middle of the length of the buckram on what is now the back of the obi. Pin in place six evenly spaced pleats across the front of the obi, each about ¾ inch wide, with the first one starting 1¼ inches down from the top of the piece and the last one 1¼ inches up from the bottom. Then turn in all excess fabric at the two sides to fit the contours of the buckram. Seam the end pieces and inconspicuously tack the pleats in place. *Ties (make two):* With size H hook, ch 12. Then work in sc on 11 sts for 2 rows, dec 1 st at beg and end of the next row, work on 9 sts for 4 rows, dec 1 st at beg and end of the next row, work on 7 sts for 4 more rows, dec 1 st again at beg and end of the next row, and then work even on 5 sts until entire piece measures 39 inches. Finally, dec 1 st at beg of the next row and every other row until 1 st remains and fasten off. With size C hook, work 1 row of sc around piece and then sew the wide part of each tie to an end of the fabric portion of the obi.

An Envelope Bag for On or Off the Shoulder

Richly textured, this 10-inch x 13½-inch envelope bag is crocheted with a straw novelty yarn in a simple pattern stitch. The strap, also made of straw, can be either hung over the shoulder or tucked inside the bag.

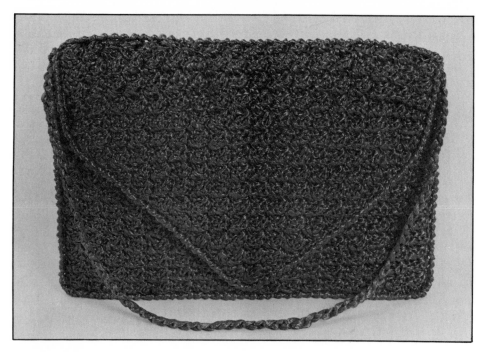

Materials

10 balls (50 grams each) lightweight straw or other novelty yarn in red
½ yard lining fabric, 36 inches wide, in red
½ yard stiff buckram, 36 inches wide
aluminum crochet hook, size G
1 snap fastener

Pattern Stitch: Row 1: Ch 2, 1 sc and 1 dc in third ch from hook, *skip 2 ch, 1 sc and 2 dc in next ch, rep from * across the row, and end with 1 sc in last ch, ch 1, and turn. *Row 2:* *1 sc and 2 dc in next sc, skip 2 dc, rep from * across the row, and end with 1 sc in last ch, ch 1, and turn. Repeat Row 2 for pattern.

Gauge in Pattern Stitch: 5 stitches = 2 inches, using double yarn throughout

Purse

Using double strands of yarn, ch 55 and work even in pat st on 54 sts for 20 inches. Dec 1 st now at beg and end of every row until 2 sts remain; fasten off. *Finishing:* Cut the lining fabric and the buckram to fit the crocheted piece, allowing ¼ inch extra all around on the lining fabric for a hem. Sew the hem, and then stitch the lining to the crocheted portion, fitting the buckram between the two layers. Finally, fold the straight 13½-inch edge up 8 inches (leaving the remainder for the flap) and seam the side edges together. Work 1 row of sc around the entire piece, working through the two thicknesses along the side edges. Then work 1 more row of sc, working this round from right to left instead of from left to right. With eight strands of the yarn, crochet a chain that measures 46 inches and sl st the last ch into the first to make a circle. Stitch part of the chain across the inside of the fold marking the turnover of the flap and leave the remainder of the chain extending to make a strap. Finally, sew one part of the snap fastener to the inside of the point of the flap and the other part in corresponding position on the front of the envelope.

A Star Is Borne

Studded with royal blue rhinestones, the satin disco bag shown here is made in the shape of a star large enough to hold your lipstick, key, and a little change. It hangs from a tasseled, wrap-around-the-waist belt crocheted of silver and a shiny midnight blue yarn.

Materials

brown wrapping paper
1 satin square, 8 inches x 16 inches, in medium blue
   and 1 square in white
small amount of polyester stuffing
1 snap fastener
26 small rhinestones in royal blue
fabric glue
12 yards medium-weight yarn in silver metallic
6 yards shiny novelty yarn in royal blue
aluminum crochet hook, size F

Bag

On brown wrapping paper, enlarge the pattern, cut it out, and use it to cut four pieces, two from the blue satin and two from the white, adding 1 inch all around for a seam allowance. Work a row of stay-stitching around each piece to prevent raveling of the fabric. Then join the top portion of one blue piece with that of one white piece, working around from A to B on the pattern. Trim away the excess fabric close to the stay-stitching. Sew the other two pieces together in the same way and trim away the excess fabric. Now turn both joined pieces right side out and stuff the three joined or partially joined points and the center portion of each. Place the two stars together, white sides out, and join the remaining bottom portion, sewing through all four thicknesses of the material. Then turn the piece blue sides out and stuff the lower two points of the star. Tack the white lining pieces together to make a pocket, as shown on the pattern, and finally sew the two stars together with a whipstitch along the edges indicated by slashes on the pattern. *Finishing:* Sew the snap fastener at the top point for a closure and then glue thirteen rhinestones at random on each side of the bag. Using two strands of the metallic thread and one of the blue yarn together, crochet two chains, one 29 inches long and the other 36 inches long, for the hanging belt. Then work 1 row of single crochet along each chain, working this row into the bottom lps of the chain. Sew one end of one chain to point A on the pattern; sew one end of the other chain to point B. Finally, make two tassels, one to be sewn to each free end of the chain as follows: Cut several strands of the metallic and the blue yarn, each 6 inches long, and tie them together, through the center, with a strand of silver yarn. Fold the strands in half and tie another silver strand around the bundle 1 inch below the folded top; sew the tassels in place. For additional trim, wrap about ¼ yard of the silver yarn around the points where the tassels were attached.

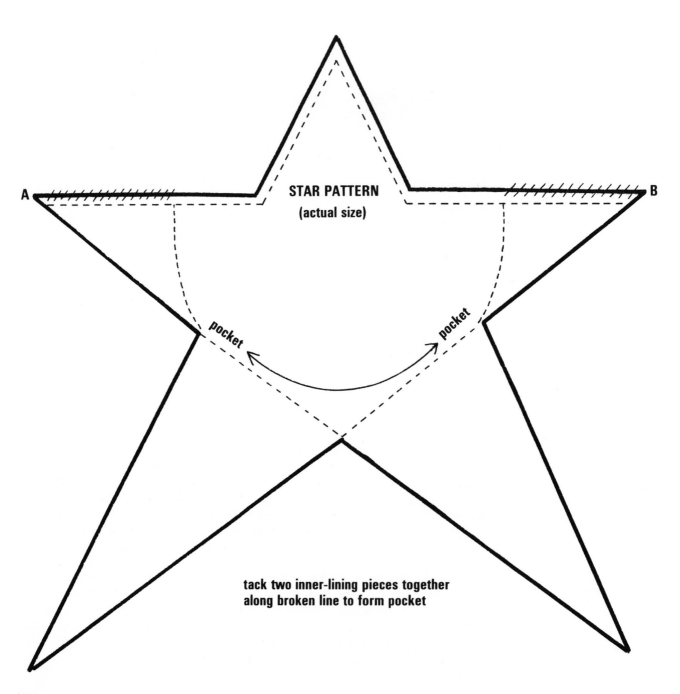

A
B

STAR PATTERN
(actual size)

pocket

pocket

**tack two inner-lining pieces together
along broken line to form pocket**

Book Tote

Since paperback books have a way of wearing out fast, why not protect yours in this handy, easy-to-carry, knitted tote, which is also a very handsome accessory. The size of the book we've used here is 4½ inches x 7½ inches, but in the instructions you will learn how to make the tote larger or smaller to accommodate different sizes of books.

Materials

2 ounces knitting worsted in each of copper, black, and white
3 pieces cotton velvet, one 8 inches x 15 inches and two 1¾ inches x 8 inches, in copper
straight knitting needles, No. 8
aluminum crochet hook, size H

Pattern Stitch: Row 1: *K 1, sl 1, rep from * across the row. *Row 2:* *P 1, sl 1, rep from * across the row. Repeat Rows 1 and 2 for the pattern, starting with copper, working the next row in black, the next in white, and rotating these three colors in that sequence on every row throughout.

Gauge in Pattern Stitch: 5 stitches = 1 inch

Tote

With copper, cast on 34 sts, or the number of sts to equal the height of the book you're most likely to be carrying. Working even throughout, work in copper stockinette st for 5 rows. Then, continuing the first and last 5 sts in copper stockinette st, work in pat on the center 24 sts, starting with Row 2 and black yarn. Continue in this way, maintaining pat as now established, until piece measures 8 inches from the start of the pattern stitch, or the desired number of inches less the inches added by the 10 rows of copper stockinette sts (starting and ending borders) to accommodate the width of the book you want to cover. End the three-color pattern stitch in copper. Then work 5 rows of copper stockinette st and bind off. *Finishing:* Work 2 rows of copper single crochet around the entire outer edge of the piece, working 3 sc in each corner stitch as you turn. Fold the two narrow strips of velvet in thirds the long way so that the edges are in the center and overcast together the edges to make the handles. Center and wrap the large piece of velvet around the width of the open book to be covered, right side out. Turn the extensions on each side to the inside of the cover to make flaps; stitch them in place along the top and bottom edges. Then, seams inside, sew one of the handles to the top of each of the folds on the long book edges, overlapping about ¼ inch on the outside of the piece (each end should be about 2 inches in from an outer corner). Block the knitted piece, lay it over the right side of the velvet cover so that it covers the ends of the handles, and stitch it in place around the four outside edges. With double strands of copper, crochet two chains, one long enough to divide the copper stockinette st borders from the pat st center portion and one to divide the 2 sc rows around the outer edge from the stockinette st. Sew the chains in place.

Quilted Calico Carryall

Our carryall, which measures approximately 12 inches x 16 inches, is a gay and handy item to have for doing the marketing, going to the beach, taking the baby for an outing, or any other time when it's necessary to tote things along.

Materials

1 yard reversible prequilted calico, 36 inches wide, in red
¼ yard lining fabric, 36 inches wide, in black
3 yards hem facing, ⅝ inch wide, in black
3 strips medium-weight cardboard, two 3 inches x 10 inches and
   one 3 inches x 16 inches
1 button, 1¼ inches in diameter, in black

Carryall

From the calico, cut one piece measuring 6 inches x 16½ inches for the flap, one piece 16½ inches x 25 inches for the main part of the bag, two 4-inch x 11½-inch pieces for the gussets, and two 2½-inch x 36-inch pieces for the straps. Seam the flap to the main body piece of the bag, allowing for ½-inch seams on the wrong side of the work for this joining and all other seams except on the straps. Turn under a ½-inch hem at the lower edge of the flap and the corresponding upper edge of the main body piece. Then fit and sew the gusset strip in place along each side of the main body piece. Now fold the two strap pieces in half lengthwise, stitch them ⅜ inch in from the open long edge, and then seam the four short ends of the straps together to form one continuous piece. Fold the hem facing in half over the one long and two short edges of the flap and along both long edges of the strap and stitch in place. Make a 3-inch button loop of the same material and sew it in place to the wrong side of the center of the lower edge of the flap. *Finishing:* Cover the cardboard pieces with lining material, seam the lining material in place, and then sew these three pieces to the inside of the bag, seam sides concealed against the inside of the bag, along the bottom of the bag and the two gusset strips. Sew the button in place to correspond to the button loop. Finally, position the strap along each side of the bag 4 inches in from the side-gusset seams and tack it in place on the bottom of the bag, about 4 inches down from the top of the front of the bag, and in a corresponding position on the back.

A Rainbow-striped Sleeveless Pullover

Crocheted in an interesting, textured stitch, this minivest, designed for small (32–34), medium (36–38), and large (40–42) sizes, just nips the waist, although it can be made longer by continuing with the sequence of stripes. It has enough colors—eight bright ones—in it that it will go with nearly anything you want to wear it with.

Materials

2 (4, 4) ounces knitting worsted yarn in navy (A) and 2 (3, 4) ounces in each of royal blue (B), medium blue (C), scarlet (D), orange (E), bright yellow (F), kelly green (G), and bottle green (H)
aluminum crochet hooks, sizes F, G, and J

Pattern Stitches: Front Post Double Crochet: Yo, insert hook from back to front to back around post of next dc on previous row, yo, draw through, and complete stitch as for a regular dc. *Back Post Double Crochet:* Work as for front post dc, but insert the hook from front to back to front.

Gauge in Single Crochet: 3 stitches and 4 rows = 1 inch on size J hook

Pullover

Back: With color A and size G hook, ch 52 (58, 64) sts. Work a border pattern stitch as follows: *Row 1 (wrong side):* 1 sc in second ch from hook, *1 dc in next ch, 1 sc in next, rep from * across the row, ch 1, and turn. *Row 2:* 1 sc in first sc, *1 front post dc, 1 sc in next sc, rep from * across the row, ch 1, and turn. *Row 3:* 1 sc in first sc, *1 back post dc, 1 sc in next sc, rep from * across the row, ch 1, and turn. Rep Row 2 once more, and then change to size J hook; work in sc across the next row. *Next row:* Change to color B and work in sc through the back lps only of the sts. *Next row:* With B, work in sc in the usual way. Continuing now to alternate 1 row of sc through the back lps only and 1 row of sc worked in the usual way and working in a color sequence of 2 rows each of B, C, D, E, F, G, H, and A, work even until piece measures 15 (16, 17) inches or the desired length above the top of the color A bottom border; fasten off.

Front: Work as for back until piece measures 4 (4½, 4½) inches above the bottom border, ending with a wrong-side row. *Shape neck:* Continuing to maintain color sequence throughout, work to within center 9 (11, 13) sts, ch 1, and turn. Working on these sts only, work 1 row even on 21 (23, 25) sts, dec 1 st at neck edge every other row until there are 19 (21, 23) sts, and work even on these sts until piece is same length as back; fasten off. Then return to row where neck shaping began, skip center 9 (11, 13) sts, attach yarn, and work the other side to correspond, reversing the shaping.

Finishing: Sew shoulder and side seams, leaving an 8 (8¼, 8½)-inch opening at each side for the armholes. With size F hook and color A, work 1 row of sc around the neck and armhole edges. Change to size G hook and work 2 rows of the bottom border pattern stitch around each of these edges.

Light and Lacy, A Shawl for Cool Evenings

Crocheted on a large hook, our lightweight but warm mohair shawl is worked in an open pattern stitch in the cool colors of off-white, sea green, and sky blue. Its finished size, including the fringe at each end, measures 36 inches x 72 inches, ample enough to ward off the chill of a late-summer evening or to wrap up in by an ebbing fire on a wintry night.

Materials

5 balls (50 grams each) lightweight mohair yarn in off-white (A)
**   and 2 balls in each of sea green (B) and sky blue (C)**
aluminum crochet hook, size N

Pattern Stitch: Row 1: Ch 3, 2 dc in fourth ch from hook, *skip 2 ch, (sl st, ch 3, and 2 dc) in next ch, rep from * across the row, and end with a sl st in the last ch, ch 3, and turn. *Row 2:* 2 dc in first sl st, *skip 2 dc, (sl st, ch 3, and 2 dc) in next ch-3 sp, rep from * across the row, and end with a sl st in the turning ch of the previous row, ch 3, and turn. Repeat Row 2 for pattern.

Gauge in Pattern Stitch: 7 stitches = 3 inches

Shawl

Starting with A, ch 133. Then working in pat st throughout on 132 sts. work 6 rows A, 4 rows B, 4 rows A, 4 rows C, 4 rows A, 4 rows B, and 2 rows A; fasten off. *Finishing:* To form a shawl collar, place the shawl so that the wide off-white stripe is at the top. Working from the center back of the neck to the ends of the shawl, turn over, pin, and then tack the top 6 off-white rows to the right side of the work. Fold the stripe in half at the back of the neck and then gradually taper the turnover to ¾ inch at each end. Finally, cut a number of 13-inch-long strands of each color yarn. Working color over color, knot four groups of two strands each along the short edge of each stripe and three groups along the narrower color A stripe.

Tweedy Vest

Knitted with a tweed-textured stitch, this form-fitting vest has a narrow shawl collar, points at the lower edge in traditional man's suit style, and a chain-button closing. Written for a small size (8–10), instructions for medium (12–14) and large (16–18) sizes are given in parentheses.

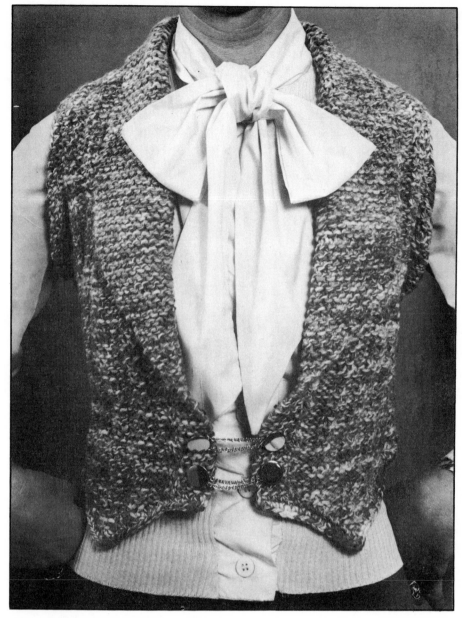

Materials

6 (8, 10) ounces knitting worsted in a random tweed mixture
straight knitting needles, No. 9
aluminum crochet hook, size H
2 button-chain fasteners
3 hooks and eyes

Pattern Stitch: Row 1 (right side): *K 2, p 2, rep from * across the row. *Row 2:* K. Repeat these 2 rows for the pattern stitch.

Gauge in Pattern Stitch: 4 stitches and 5 rows = 1 inch

Vest

Back: Cast on 50 (54, 62) sts and work even in pat st for 5 (5¾, 6½) inches. Inc 1 st now at beg and end of the next and every other row 7 (9, 9) times, being sure to maintain pat as established and adding more pattern sts as increases are made. When there are 64 (72, 80) sts, end with a wrong-side row and shape armholes: Bind off 5 (6, 7) sts at beg of each of the next 2 rows, work 1 row even, and then dec 1 st at each edge every other row 7 times. Work even on 40 (46, 52) sts until armholes measure 7 (7½, 8) inches. To shape shoulders, bind off 6 (7, 8) sts at beg of each of the next 4 rows and, finally, loosely bind off remaining 16 (18, 20) sts for back of neck.

Left front: Cast on 2 sts. *Row 1 (right side):* K 2. *Row 2:* K, increasing 1 st in each of the 2 sts (4 sts). *Row 3:* K, increasing 1 st in the first and last sts (6 sts). *Row 4:* K, increasing 1 st in first and last sts (8 sts). *Row 5:* Inc 1 st in first st, p 2, k 2, p 2, inc 1 st in last st (10 sts). Now continue pat as established, increasing 1 st at beg and end of every row until there are 18 (20, 24) sts in all. Continuing to maintain pat as established and adding more pattern sts as increases are made, inc 1 st at side edge only on every row until there are 24 (26, 30) sts; then work even for 5 (5¾, 6½) inches more. Now inc 1 st at side edge every other row 7 (9, 9) times, and *at the same time,* after the third inc has been made, start to shape neck: Dec 1 st at front edge and at same edge every sixth row 6 (7, 8) times more. Continuing to inc as necessary on opposite edge, when piece measures same as back to start of armhole shaping, shape armhole as on back. Then work even until armhole measures ½-inch longer than back armhole. Shape shoulder as on back. *Right front:* Work as for left front, reversing all shaping.

Finishing: Collar and lower front bands: Cast on 5 sts and work even in garter st (all knit) for 4 (4¾, 6½) inches. Then inc 1 st on one edge only on every other row until there are 14 sts in all. Work even now on 14 sts for 23 (24½, 26) inches more and then dec 1 st every other row on same edge as increases were made until 5 sts remain. Work even for 4 (4¾, 5½) inches more and then bind off. Sew side and shoulder seams; sew collar and front bands in place. Work 2 rows of single crochet around the lower edge of the vest, working 3 sc in each front point, and 1 row around each armhole. Finally, sew on the three hook-and-eye fasteners, spacing them evenly along the front border and placing them so that the two finished center edges are positioned edge to edge. Then sew on the two button-chain fasteners, spacing them evenly, as shown in the photograph.

A Gathered-at-the-Waist Tyrolean Sweater

Whether you wear this knitted sweater for fashion or warmth, you'll be happy with the appearance it makes alone or over a long-sleeved blouse or a lighter-weight sweater. Made of a bulky yarn, on large needles, our sweater is colorful and different-looking. Although the instructions are for a small size (32–34), there are, in parentheses, changes for medium (36–38) and large (40–42) sizes.

Materials

5 (6, 7) balls (4 ounces each) bulky yarn in off-white (MC) and
   1 ball each in scarlet (A) and forest green (B)
straight knitting needles, No. 13
aluminum crochet hooks, sizes G and H
5 buttons, each ⅞ inch in diameter, in silver
1 snap fastener

Gauge in Reverse Stockinette Stitch: 5 stitches = 2 inches

Sweater

Back: With MC, cast on 43 (47, 51) sts. Work in reverse stockinette st (p 1 row—right side, k 1 row) for 3 (3, 3½) inches and then work a beading row as follows: K 3, *yo, k 2 tog, k 2, rep from * across the row. On the next row, p each st and each yo—43 (47, 51) sts. Work even now in reverse stockinette st until piece measures 9 (9½, 10) inches, or desired length, above the beading row. *Shape armholes:* Bind off 2 sts at beg of each of the next 2 rows and then dec 1 st at each edge every other row twice. Now work even on 35 (39, 43) sts until piece measures 7¼ (7¾, 8¼) inches above the start of the armhole shaping, ending with a wrong-side row. *To shape shoulders,* bind off 6 sts at beg of the next 2 rows, 5 (6, 7) sts at the beg of the next 2 rows, and then loosely bind off the remaining 13 (15, 17) sts for the back of the neck. *Left front:* With MC, cast on 21 (23, 25) sts and then work in reverse stockinette st for 3 inches. Work a beading row as on the back and then work even until piece measures same as back to the start of the armhole shaping, ending at the side edge. Shape the armhole as on the back and *at the same time,* when piece measures 1½ (2, 2½) inches above the armhole, begin to shape the neck: At the front edge, bind off 3 sts and then dec 1 st at same edge every other row 3 (4, 5) times. Now work even on remaining sts until piece measures same as back to shoulders; shape shoulder as on back. *Right front:* Work to correspond to left front, reversing the shaping. *Finishing:* Sew side and shoulder seams. With MC and size G hook, work 1 row of sc along all outer edges, then 1 row of color A, 3 rows MC, and 1 row color B, decreasing 1 st in every third st on the last rnd of MC and in every sixth st on the color B rnd on the neck and armhole edges only and at the same time working in five buttonholes on the right front on the third MC row, the first one 1 inch above the beading row, the last one 1 inch below the top of the neck and the remaining three spaced evenly between. To make buttonholes, work in sc until reaching the position for the buttonhole and then ch 1, skip 1 sc, and sc in the next sc; on the return row, work 1 sc in each sc and in each ch-1 space. Embroider the crocheted band now, as shown, by working 1 row of color A running chain st over the inside MC crocheted row, 1 row of color B on the inside of the center MC row, and 1 row color A on the outside of the center MC row. Finish the trim by working a row of MC French knots spaced approximately 1 inch apart over the center MC row, between the color B and color A running chains. Complete the sweater by making, with double strands of MC and the size H hook, a chain approximately 60-inches long. Draw it through the beading row and make and fasten a small MC pompom at each end of the chain. Sew the snap fastener at the neck edge for a more complete closure.

A Soft and Furry Dolman Slipover

Designed in the perennially popular Dolman style–a special favorite these days–the vari-striped sweater here is knitted in a soft mohair that accentuates its butterfly-wing-like sleeves. Because it's worked on very large, number 15 needles, it can be made in practically no time at all. Instructions are given for a small size with changes for medium and large given in parentheses.

Materials

4 (5, 6) balls (50 grams each) medium-weight mohair in off-white (MC) and 1 ball in each of
    mulberry (A), deep red (B), and dark pink (C)
straight knitting needles, Nos. 10 and 15
round knitting needle, No. 10 ·

Gauge in Stockinette Stitch: 5 stitches = 2 inches

126

Slipover

Starting at the bottom front, with No. 10 needles and MC, cast on 42 (46, 50) sts. Work in k 1, p 1 ribbing for 3 inches. Change to No. 15 needles and stockinette st (k 1 row, p 1 row) and work even for 2 inches, at the same time working the stripe pat as follows: 2 (4, 6) rows MC, 6 rows A, 4 rows MC, 4 rows B, 4 rows MC, 2 rows C. Continue to alternate 4 rows MC and 2 rows A, B, and C to the shoulder line. When the 2 inches above the ribbing have been completed, begin to inc 1 st at beg and end of every other row until piece measures 11 inches from beg—62 (66, 70) sts—ending with a wrong-side row. Now cast on 14 (16, 18) sts at beg of next row for the left sleeve, work across the 62 (66, 70) sts on the needle, and cast on 14 (16, 18) sts for the right sleeve. Working on the 90 (98, 106) sts and continuing to maintain the stripe pat, work even for 1½ (2½, 3½) inches, ending with a wrong-side row. Then shape neck: Work to within center 8 sts, join another ball of yarn, bind off those 8 sts, and continue to work across the remaining sts. Working on both sides at the same time now, dec 1 st at each neck edge every fourth row 4 times. Work 1 row even and mark this point for the shoulder line. Continuing on for the back and reversing the stripe pat so that it corresponds to the front, shape the back of the neck as follows: Cast on 1 st at each neck edge every other row 4 times, ending with a wrong-side row. On the next row, work to the neck edge, cast on 8 sts, drop the second ball of yarn, and continue working across the row. Work now on 90 (98, 106) sts until piece measures the same length from the shoulder line to the bottom edge of sleeve as it does on the front. Then bind off 14 (16, 18) sts at beg of each of the next 2 rows and work even until piece measures the same as the front to the start of the ribbing. Change to No. 10 needles and, with MC, work in k 1, p 1 ribbing for 3 inches; then bind off loosely in ribbing. *Finishing:* With No. 10 needles and MC, pick up and k 26 (30, 34) sts around each sleeve edge, work in k 1, p 1 ribbing to 2½ inches, and bind off; then with the round needle, pick up and k 78 sts around the neck edge and work in k 1, p 1 ribbing on those sts for 1 inch. Finally, sew side and underarm sleeve seams.

Snowflake Sweater

A scattering of white snowflakes trim this pine green apres-ski or wear-it-anywhere knitted wraparound sweater-jacket. Instructions are written for a small size (10–12), with changes for medium (14–16) and large (18–20) sizes in parentheses.

Materials

4 (5, 6) balls (4 ounces each) bulky yarn in forest green and 2 (3, 3) balls in white
straight knitting needles, No. 13
large-eyed embroidery needle

Gauge in Stockinette Stitch: 12 stitches = 5 inches; 3 rows = 1 inch

Sweater

Back: With the green, cast on 40 (46, 52) sts, and work in garter st (all knit) for 2 (2½, 3) inches. Then change to stockinette st and work even for 16 inches more. Continuing now to work even, work the first and last 4 sts in garter st and the center 32 (38, 44) sts in stockinette for 4 (4½, 5) inches more. To complete the back, work across all sts in garter st for 2 (2½, 3) inches and bind off loosely. *Left front:* With the green, cast on 29 (32, 35) sts and work in garter st for 2 (2½, 3) inches. Continuing to work only the first 4 sts in green garter st now to completion of the left front for the front border, work in white stockinette st on the remaining sts for the next 7 rows, then alternate 7 rows green and 7 rows white on the stockinette sts until piece measures same as back to the point where the first and last 4 sts were worked in garter st and *at the same time* when piece measures 7 (7½, 8) inches in all, shape neck: Dec 1 st at front edge on the first 2 stockinette sts and rep this dec every fourth row 13 times more, working each dec after the garter st border and working the last two decs in the garter st section at end of piece. To complete the left front, when the fourth white stripe has been worked, work in green only and work the first and last 4 sts in garter st to the point where all sts at the top of the back are worked in garter st. Then work in all garter st until piece measures same as back completion. Bind off loosely. *Right front:* Work to correspond to left front, reversing all shaping. *Sleeves:* With green, cast on 29 (34, 39) sts and work in garter st for 2 (2½, 3) inches. Then change to stockinette st and work even until piece measures 14½ (15, 15½) inches. Bind off loosely. *Finishing:* Sew the side seams to the point of the yoke where there are the 4 garter sts at each side edge. Sew the sleeve and shoulder seams and then sew the sleeves in place, easing the tops of them into the open garter st portion. To make the belt, cast on 5 sts with green and work even in garter st for 45 (47, 49) inches; bind off. For belt loops, loop two strands of green yarn across the width of the center green stripe at each side edge and sew the ends securely in place. Finally, following the patterns and using the white yarn, embroider one large snowflake on the left yoke and three small ones at the bottom of the left sleeve just above the garter st border, as shown on page 135.

SNOWFLAKE PATTERNS (actual size)

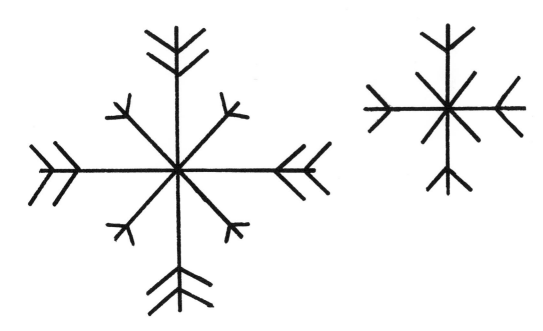

A Norwegian Mesh Pullover for Him

Crocheted and copied after a Scandinavian undershirt, this handsome mesh top is designed for small, medium, and large sizes. Made in a combination of wool and cotton it can be worn alone in warm weather or under a shirt in cold weather to hold in body heat. The directions and materials needed for the two larger sizes are in parentheses.

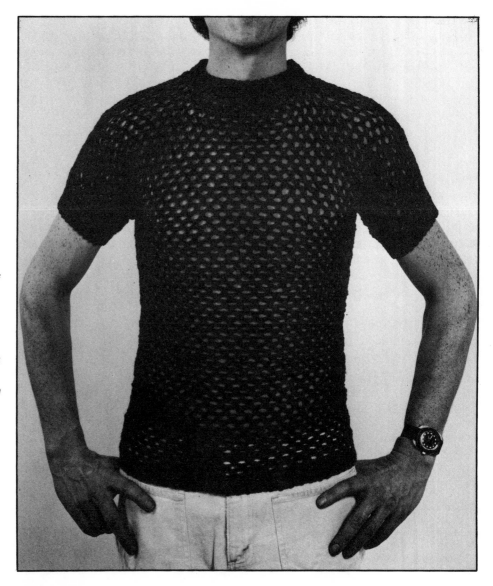

Materials

5 (6, 6) skeins (1 ounce each) sport-weight yarn in cranberry
4 (5, 5) balls (100 yards each) medium-weight mercerized cotton in black
aluminum crochet hooks, sizes F and H

Pattern Stitch: Row 1: 1 sc in first st, *ch 3, skip 2 sts, 1 sc in next st, rep from * across the row, ch 5, and turn. *Row 2:* *1 sc in second ch of next ch-3 sp, ch 3, rep from * across the row, and end with 1 sc in the second ch of the last ch-3 sp, 1 sc in next ch, ch 5, and turn. Repeat Row 2 for the pattern.

Gauge in Pattern Stitch: 3 mesh spaces = 2 inches on size H hook

Shirt

Starting at the front and using the size H hook and one strand of both the wool and the cotton together throughout, ch 74 (83, 92). Work even in pat on 73 (82, 91) sts for 14 (14½, 14½) inches. *To shape sleeves:* Ch 22 (25, 28) at end of the last row turn,work across the 21 (24, 27) sts and the 73 (82, 91) body sts, ch 22 (25, 28) at the end of the row, and turn. Working on all sts now, work even in pat until piece measures 18½ (19½, 20½) inches in all. To shape neck, work to within center 4 spaces, ch, and turn. Work on only these sts for 1 row. On the next row, work to within the last 2 spaces of the previous row, ch, and turn. Rep the last 2 rows once more and then work even on remaining sts until piece measures 6½ (7, 7½) inches above the start of the sleeve shaping; fasten off. Now join yarn again after the center 4 spaces on the row where the neck shaping began and work the other armhole and shoulder side to correspond. When the last row has been completed, ending at the neck edge, ch 36 for the back of the neck and then work in pat across the sts of the already-finished shoulder, ch, and turn. On the next row, work across the finished shoulder sts, work 12 mesh across the chain made for the back of the neck, work across the other shoulder sts, ch, and turn. Now complete the back of the sweater to correspond to the front. *Finishing:* Sew side and underarm seams. Make four strips of ribbing as follows: With size F hook and one strand of each yarn together, ch 7. Working back and forth in sc through the back lps only of the sts, make one piece 20 (21, 22) inches long for the neckband, two pieces each 10 (10½, 11) inches long for the sleeve bottoms, and one piece 28 (30, 32) inches for the bottom of the sweater; sew on the ribbings.

For Cold Weather, A Thick, Crocheted Poncho for Him or Her

Made in a bulky off-white yarn strikingly trimmed with rust and black, this very warm poncho (one size fits all) is worked almost as a crochet stitch sampler through the use of three different, very simple to work, but highly textured stitches, plus the single crochet stitch used for the trim.

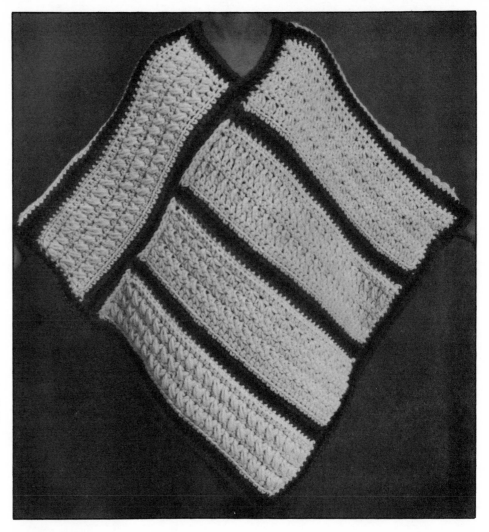

Materials

**7 skeins (4 ounces each) bulky yarn in off-white (MC) and 2 skeins in each of rust (A)
and black (B)
aluminum crochet hook, size K**

Pattern Stitch No. 1: Row 1: Keeping all lps on hook, yo, insert hook in first sc, *(yo and draw through, yo, insert hook in same sc, yo and draw through), skip 1 sc, yo, insert hook in next sc, rep step in parentheses once, yo and draw through 9 lps on hook, ch 1, yo, insert hook in last skipped st, rep from * across the row, and end by repeating step in parentheses once, (yo, insert hook in last st, yo and draw through) twice, yo and draw through 9 lps on hook, ch 1, and turn. *Row 2:* *1 sc in next ch-1 sp, 1 sc in next st, rep from * across the row, ch 3, and turn. Repeat Rows 1 and 2 for pattern stitch No. 1.

Pattern Stitch No. 2: Row 1: Keeping all lps on hook, (insert hook in second ch from hook, yo and draw through), insert hook in next ch, yo and draw through, insert hook in first st, yo and draw through, insert hook in next st, yo and draw through, yo

Left to right: *Strictly for After Dark, A Sequined Cap and Scarf Duet,* p. 96; *A Versatile Obi Sash,* p. 110; *Personalized, An Oversized Beret Knitted of Mohair,* p. 98; *A Long, Skinny Boa,* p. 99; *A Star is Borne,* p. 113.

Above, left to right: *Star-sprinkled Helmet, Dickey, and Mitten Set,*
p.70; A Fringy Fashion Jacket, p.86; A Winter-white Pram Suit,
p. 18; Light and Lacy, A Shawl for Cool Evenings, p. 120.

Opposite top: *A Gathered-at-the-Waist Tyrolean Sweater, p. 124;*
Snowflake Sweater, p. 128.

Opposite bottom, left to right: *Plaid Scarf Knitted in Tartan*
Colors, p. 100; A Cap, Scarf, and Leg-warmer Set Trimmed with Bolts
of Lightning, p. 104; Flower-embroidered Poncho-in-the-Round,
p. 139.

Baby Carriers—One for Him and One for Her, p. 29.

and draw through 5 lps on hook, *ch 1, and then, keeping all lps on hook, insert hook in ch-1 sp just made, yo and draw through, insert hook in the last st worked before yo and drawing through 5 loops, yo and draw through (insert hook in next sc, yo, and draw through) twice, yo and draw through 5 lps on hook, rep from * across the row, ch 3, and turn. *Row 2:* Keeping all lps on hook, insert hook in second ch from hook, yo and draw through, insert hook in next ch, yo and draw through, insert hook in first ch-1 sp of previous row, yo and draw through, insert hook in next st, yo and draw through, yo and draw through all 5 lps on hook, ch 1, *insert hook in ch-1 sp just made, yo and draw through, insert hook in last st worked on this row, yo and draw through, insert hook in next ch-1 sp, yo and draw through, insert hook in next st, yo and draw through all 5 lps on hook, ch 1, rep from * across the row, ch 3, and turn. Repeat Row 2 for pattern stitch No. 2.

Pattern Stitch No. 3: Row 1: Ch 2, work 1 dc in first st and in each st across, ch 1, and turn. *Row 2:* Work 1 sc in each dc, ch 2, and turn. *Row 3:* *Skip 1 sc, yo, insert hook horizontally from right to left under dc 1 row below skipped sc (do not count turning ch-2 as a dc), yo and draw up a long lp, yo and draw through 3 lps on hook, 1 dc in next sc, rep from * across the row, ch 1, and turn. Repeat Rows 1 through 3 for pattern stitch No. 3.

Gauge in Single Crochet: 2 stitches = 1 inch

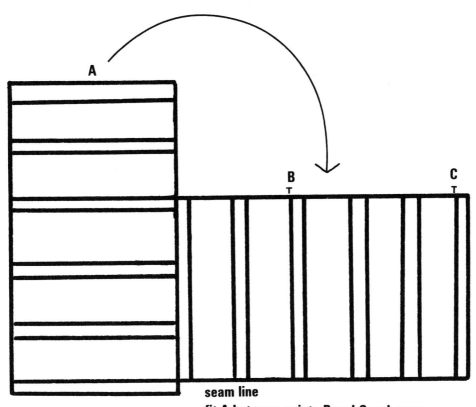

seam line
fit A between points B and C and seam

Poncho

Make two pieces: *With A, ch 45. Work in sc across 44 sts and fasten off. Return to start of row, attach B, work 1 sc in each sc across, and fasten off. Return again to start of row, attach A again, and work 1 sc in each sc; fasten off. Return once again to start of row, attach MC, work 1 row of sc, ch 1, turn, and then work 1 row of sc through the front lps only of the sts, chaining 3 to turn at the end of the row.* Now work 6 rows of pat st No. 1 and then 1 row of sc on 44 sts, working through the back lps only of the sts; fasten off. Now rep between *'s to add a stripe. Start pat st No. 2 now, working Row 1 once and then Row 2 four times, chaining 1 st to turn at the end of the last row. Then work 1 row of sc and another row of sc through the back lps only of the sts. Again rep between *'s to add a stripe and then start pattern st No. 3, working Rows 1 through 3 twice. Then work 1 row of sc and another row of sc through the back lps only of the sts. Add another stripe by repeating between *'s. To finish the panel, work pat st No. 2 and then No. 1 with 2 rows of MC sc, the second of which is worked through the back lps only, and a stripe between the two sections; finally, end the piece with a stripe, ending with the final color A row.

Finishing: Complete the poncho by working a row of color-over-color sc along the length of each panel, working 12 sc, evenly spaced, along the edge of each pattern-stitch panel. Then sew the two panels together as shown on the diagram. Finally, crochet an A-B-A finishing stripe along the unstriped bottom and neck edges, overlapping and sewing the stripe ends together at the front and back neck and seaming the stripe ends together on the bottom edge.

Flower-embroidered Poncho-in-the-Round

Cut in the round from a heavy-weight navy wool, our poncho is gaily embroidered with bright yarns and patterned so that one size fits all.

Materials

brown wrapping paper
2 yards heavy-weight wool, 60 inches wide, in navy
7 yards jersey seam binding, 1 inch wide, in navy
1 ball (4 ounces) bulky yarn in each of yellow, red, white, and bright green
large-eyed embroidery needle

Poncho

On the brown wrapping paper, enlarge the poncho pattern and cut it out. Place it on the fold of the fabric and cut around it, cutting a slit in the center through both layers of fabric for the neck opening as indicated. Sew the seam binding around the entire outer edge of the piece and around the neck opening. Transfer the embroidery pattern to the poncho, following the placement diagram for positioning and repeating the pattern as many times as necessary. Following the pattern for stitches and colors, work the embroidery to completion.

EMBROIDERY PLACEMENT DIAGRAM

Color and Stitch Key:
Flowers = lazy daisy stitch in red
Border stitches = straight stitch in green
Flower centers = French knots alternating in white and yellow beginning with white in center front flower

EMBROIDERY PATTERN

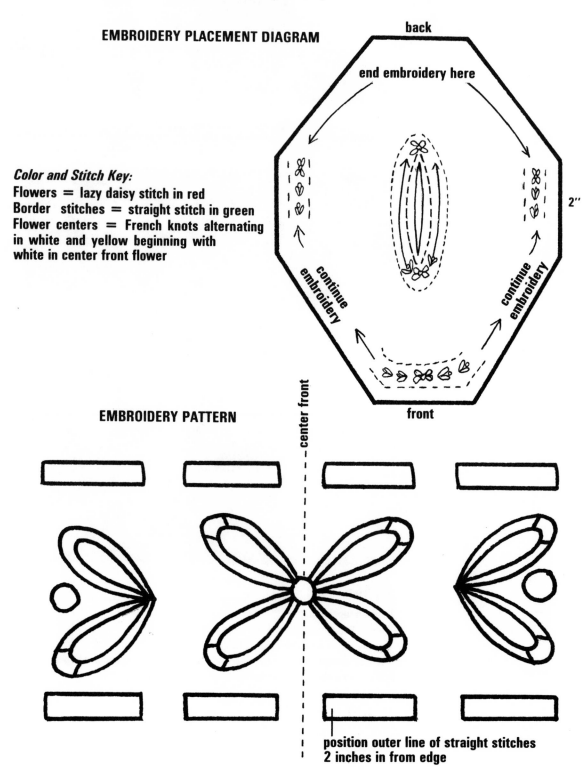

position outer line of straight stitches 2 inches in from edge

PONCHO PATTERN

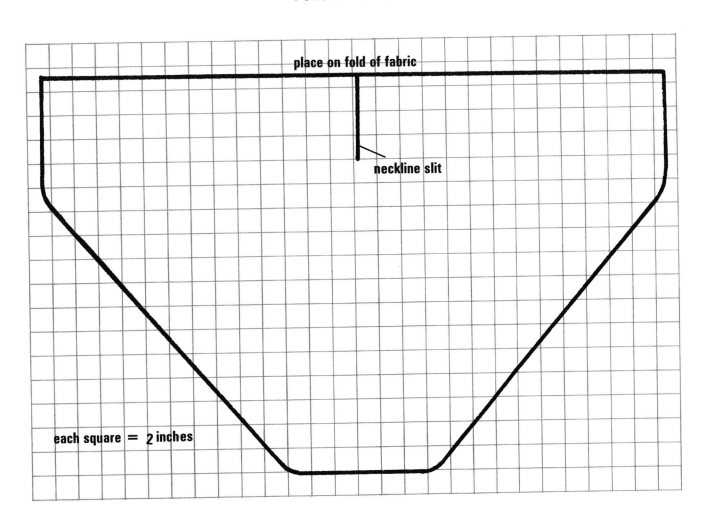

place on fold of fabric

neckline slit

each square = 2 inches

Pansy-sprigged Desk Accessories

Surprisingly, a piece of cardboard, a twelve-ounce soda can, a pair of metal book standards, and a few random materials are all that's needed to make this charming and very elegant-looking three-piece desk set.

Materials

½ yard heavy cotton velvet, 36 inches wide, in brown
felt scraps in pink, white, and black
1 piece felt, 16 inches x 24 inches, in brown
2 yards braid, 1 inch wide, in brown
small amount embroidery floss in spring green
1 piece medium-weight cardboard, 16 inches x 24 inches
desk blotter, 16 inches x 24 inches, in white
2 standard metal bookends, 5 inches square
empty soda can, 12-ounce size
white glue
household cement

Blotter

From the brown velvet, cut two strips, each 5 inches x 18 inches. Trace the pattern pieces for the large and small pansies, tracing each petal separately; cut out the pieces, cutting those portions of the petals that will overlap each other slightly larger. Lay the pieces on the felt scraps, following the pattern instructions for colors, and cut them out, cutting enough pieces for one large pansy and two small ones. Assemble each flower according to the patterns and glue them together. Now, using the brown felt as a backing, lay the cardboard over it and then lay the blotter on top of the cardboard. Lay one of the 5-inch x 18-inch velvet strips across each short end of the blotter, positioning each so that it overlaps the three outer edges of the blotter by 1 inch. Sandwich the top and bottom extensions between the felt and the cardboard and sew the felt to the velvet along the fold. Wrap the remaining extension around the felt backing and sew it in place, clipping the corners as necessary so that the work will lie flat. Cut two 17-inch lengths of braid, hem each end ½ inch to prevent raveling, and glue each along the inner edge of a velvet strip. Glue the three pansies in place as shown in the photograph. For stems, cut one 5-inch and two 2½-inch pieces of embroidery floss; arrange and glue them in place.

Bookends

From the brown velvet, cut two strips, each measuring 5¾ inches x 13 inches. Then, from the felt scraps, cut and assemble pieces for four small pansies, following the instructions for the flowers with the blotter. Fold the first 5 inches of the length of each strip over, wrong sides together, and sew the doubled side edges together with an overcast stitch. Slip each over a bookend so that the extended 3-inch portions are to the outside of the bookends. Cut two 6¾-inch lengths of braid, hem ½ inch at each end to prevent raveling, and glue each strip across the top of the outside of a bookend. Position two of the flowers, each with a 3-inch embroidery floss "stem," on each bookend as shown in the photograph and glue them in place. Finally, turn the excess velvet under each bookend and cement in place to the metal.

Pencil Holder

From the brown velvet, cut one strip 6½ inches x 9 inches and one disk 2½ inches in diameter. Then, from the felt scraps, cut and assemble pieces for two small pansies, following the instructions for the flowers with the blotter. Remove one end of the soda can and wrap the outside of the can with the strip of velvet, seaming the edges together. Then turn 1 inch of the velvet to the inside of the can at the top and ½ inch at the bottom and cement in place, clipping the bottom as necessary so that it lies flat. Next, sew the velvet disk on the bottom of the can to the turnunder. Finally, cut a 10-inch strip of braid, hem ½ inch of each end to prevent raveling, and glue it around the top of the can. Trim the finished piece by gluing on the pansies with "stems," as on the bookends.

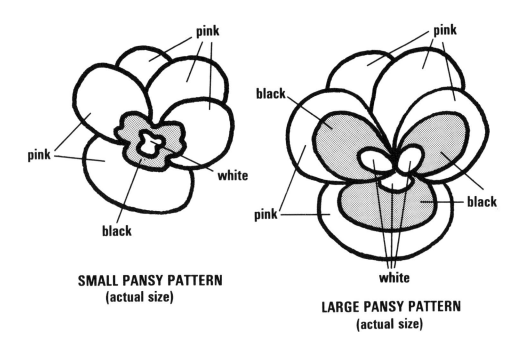

SMALL PANSY PATTERN
(actual size)

LARGE PANSY PATTERN
(actual size)

Needlework Techniques

The pages that follow show you the "how-to" involved in the working out of the knitting, crocheting, and embroidering of the simple stitches used in the re-creating of the designs in this book. Sewing techniques, however, have been purposely eliminated, since the stitches used in the sewing projects are just those very basic ones that anyone who has sewn at all knows from the early days of her grade-school home economics class.

How to Knit

It is rather amazing that this age-old and ever-popular art involves the use of only two stitches and that it is from these stitches that anything from the simplest to the most intricate patterns can be worked. Of these two, one is the *knit* stitch, the other the *purl*. Beyond this, it is necessary only to know how to cast on to start your knitting, how to bind off to complete it, and how to increase, decrease, and pick up stitches to shape and finish a garment.

Knitting

Casting On

For your first stitch, make a slip loop on the needle, allowing a two-yard end of yarn for every 100 stitches that are to be cast on, more if the yarn is a heavier-than-average weight and less if it is lighter. Holding the needle in your right hand with the short end of the yarn toward you, *make a loop on your left thumb with the short end (A). Insert the needle from front to back through this loop (B), then place the yarn attached to the ball under and around the needle (C), draw the yarn through the loop, and pull the short end down to tighten it (D). Repeat from * for the desired number of stitches.

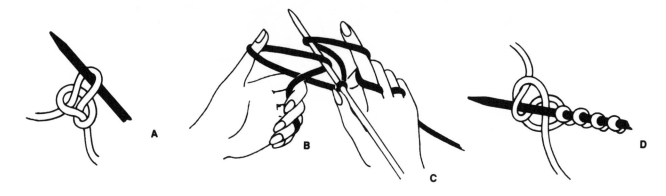

Knitting

Holding the needle with the cast-on stitches in your left hand with the yarn to the back of the work, *insert the needle in your right hand from the left to right through the front of the first stitch, wrap the yarn completely around the right needle to form a loop, slip the needle and loop through the stitch, and then slip the stitch just worked off the left needle. Repeat from * across all the stitches on the left needle.

Purling

*Holding the yarn in front of the work, insert the right needle from right to left through the front of the first stitch on the left needle, wrap the yarn completely around the right needle to form a loop, and slip the stitch just worked off the left needle. Repeat from * across all the stitches on the left needle.

Binding Off

Knit the first 2 stitches, *insert the point of the left needle into the first stitch on the right needle (A), lift this stitch over the second stitch, and then drop it off the needle (B). Repeat from * across the necessary number of stitches to be bound off. When all the stitches are to be bound off at the end of a piece of work and just one stitch remains, break off the yarn and draw the remaining strand through the stitch. All binding off should be done very loosely so that there is a sufficient amount of elasticity to the finished edge.

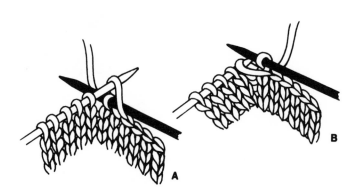

Increasing

Insert the right needle from right to left through the back of the next stitch on the left needle, then wrap the yarn completely around the needle to form a loop (A), slip the needle and loop through to the front (thus forming a new stitch on the right needle), and then knit the same stitch on the left needle in the usual manner (B). Slip the stitch off the left needle.

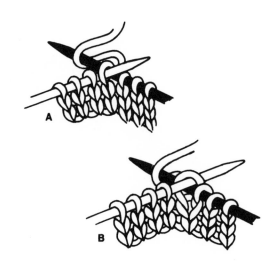

146

Decreasing

Insert the right needle through 2 stitches on the left needle and work these 2 stitches together as one.

Picking up Stitches

Picking up stitches—often necessary around a neck or an armhole—is always done on the right side of the work and is usually started at a seam edge, such as the top of one shoulder for the neck

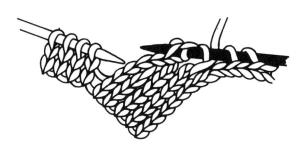

How to Crochet

The basic chain, slip stitch, single crochet, half double crochet, double crochet, and triple crochet stitches are the ones involved in the making of some of the projects in this book. Here are the working techniques of these stitches, in addition to the "how to" of increasing and decreasing, a knowledge of which is necessary for the shaping of a garment.

Foundation Chain

Knot a loop onto the hook. Holding the hook in your right hand and the end of the yarn extending from the loop between the thumb and middle finger of your left hand, loop the yarn to be worked over the index finger of your left hand. The balance of that yarn should extend from the same hand, lightly held in control between the ring and little fingers. Then *pass the hook under the extending yarn nearest to the hook and draw both the hook and the yarn through the loop already on the hook (the first stitch). Repeat from * for as many stitches as the instructions specify. (Note: Turning chains are worked in the same way as are chain stitches indicated in a pattern stitch—the last loop worked is the one through which the yarn and hook of the next stitch are drawn.)

Slip Stitch

Insert the hook through the two upper strands of the stitch to be worked, place the yarn over the hook, and then draw both yarn and the hook through the stitch and through the last loop on the hook.

Single Crochet

Insert the hook through the two upper strands of the stitch to be worked, place the yarn over the hook and draw it through the stitch, then yarn over again and draw it through the remaining two loops on the hook. When working the first row of the single crochet on a foundation chain, start your first stitch in the second chain from the hook and always chain 1 to turn when the first stitch on the next row is to be a single crochet.

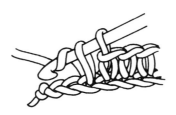

Half Double Crochet

Place the yarn over the hook and then insert the hook through the two upper strands of the stitch to be worked. Draw the yarn through the stitch, yarn over again, and draw it through the remaining three loops on the hook. When working the first row of half double crochet on a foundation chain, start your first stitch in the third chain from the hook and always chain 2 to turn when the first stitch on the next row is to be a half double crochet.

Double Crochet

Place the yarn over the hook and then insert the hook through the two upper strands of the stitch to be worked. Draw the yarn through the stitch, yarn over, draw it through two loops on the hook, yarn over again, and draw it through the remaining two loops on the hook. When working the first row of double crochet on a foundation chain, start your first stitch in the third chain from the hook and always chain 2 to turn when the first stitch on the next row is to be a double crochet.

Triple Crochet

Place the yarn twice over the hook and then insert the hook through the two upper strands of the stitch to be worked. Draw the yarn through the stitch, place the yarn over the hook, and draw it through two loops on the hook three times. When working the first row of triple crochet on a foundation chain, start your first stitch in the fourth chain from the hook and always chain 3 to turn when the first stitch on the next row is to be a triple crochet.

Increasing and Decreasing

When it is necessary to increase in a single crochet stitch, the basic formula is to work 2 stitches in the same stitch, thus forming an extra stitch. The new stitch would also be worked in single crochet, since a new stitch is always worked in the same type of stitch as the original in which the increase is being made. In double crochet, for example, the stitch to be increased would be worked in double crochet, and in triple crochet it would be a triple crochet. To decrease in single crochet, work off 2 stitches as one, thus decreasing, or "losing," a stitch. Do this by drawing up a loop in the next single crochet, then draw up another loop in the following single crochet, wrap the yarn over the hook and draw it through all three loops at once. Again, since the same stitch pattern is always maintained, as in increasing, to decrease a double crochet stitch, work your first double crochet to the point where two loops remain on the hook, then yarn over and insert the hook in the next stitch, yarn over and draw through the stitch, yarn over and draw through two loops, yarn over and draw through the remaining three loops.

How to Embroider

Shown below are the six simple embroidery stitches used throughout the book for the embellishment of some of the projects. You will find both the drawings and explanations helpful towards working out any of the stitches that are new to you.

Straight Stitch

Bring thread through at (A) along a traced or other established line and pass the needle through the fabric at (B). Continue to work in this manner.

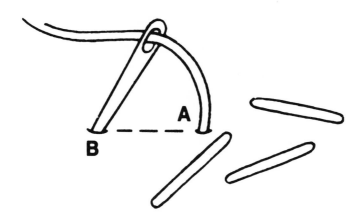

Outline Stitch or Stem Stitch

Bring the thread through at point (A) on a traced line and then pass the needle through the fabric from (B) to (C). Next, pass the needle through from (D) to (B). Continue working in this manner for the length desired.

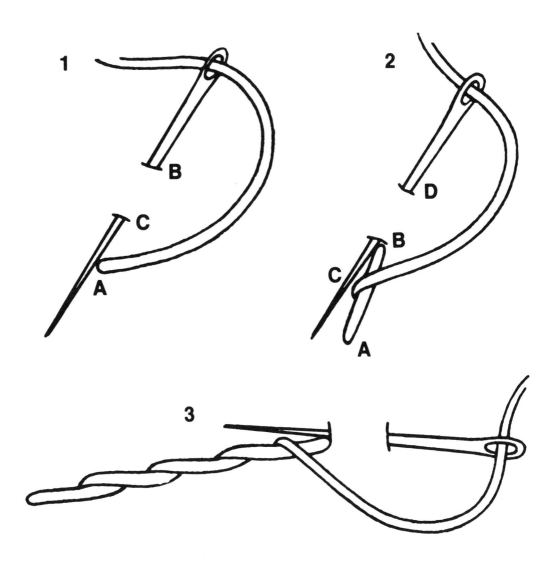

French Knot

Bring thread through from wrong to right side of the fabric at point (A) and wrap it around the needle once or as many times as desired. Then pass the needle down through the fabric again at point A. The completed stitch should look like Figure 3 below.

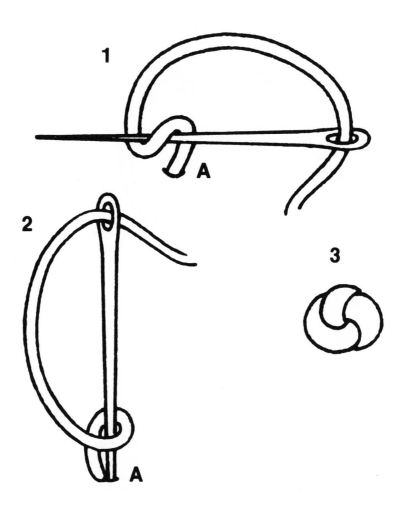

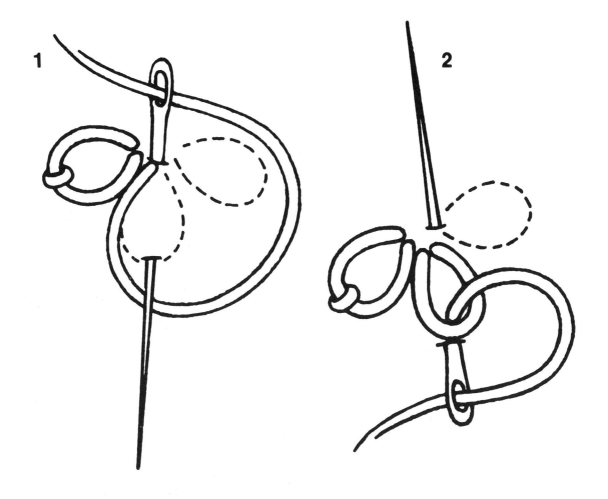

Lazy Daisy or Loop Stitch

Bring the thread through at the base of the petal on the traced line; then loop the thread around the needle and pass the needle back through the fabric, bringing it up at the center top of the petal with the thread under the needle. Make a small stitch over the loop to hold it in place, pass the needle through the fabric, and bring it up at the base of the next petal.

Running Chain Stitch

This stitch is worked along a traced or other established line. Bring the thread up through a given line at any point to be marked (A), pass the needle through from (A) to (B), and then pull it through. Continue in this manner, passing the needle through from (A) to (B), for the desired length.

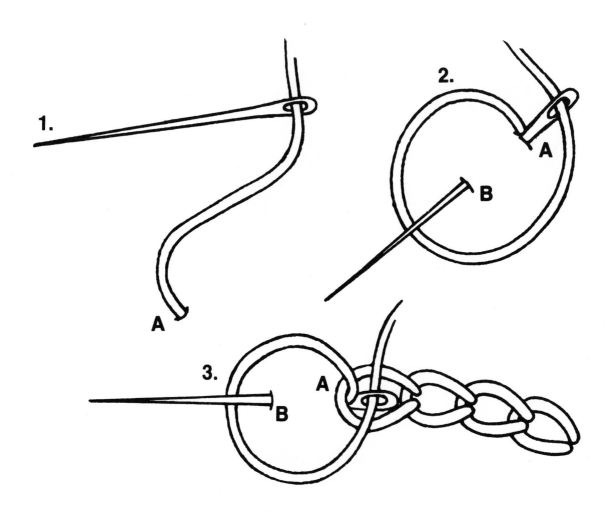

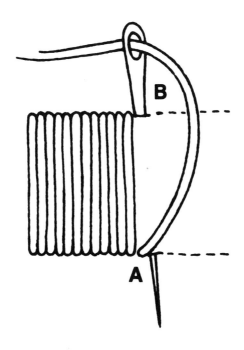

Satin Stitch

Bring the thread through at (A) along any traced or other established line. Then pass the needle down through the fabric at (B) on another established line at the opposite side of the stitch. Carry the needle across the back of the material and pass it through at the point next to (A). Continue to work in the same manner as for the first stitch.

Index

Numbers in *italics* refer to illustrations.